To Sharon
a special
Aunt Gert
Uncle Bud

Blessings!!
Bud & Gertrude Hitt

Power In Ordinary People

BUD & GERTRUDE HITT

Bloomington, IN  Milton Keynes, UK

AuthorHouse™
1663 Liberty Drive, Suite 200
Bloomington, IN 47403
www.authorhouse.com
Phone: 1-800-839-8640

AuthorHouse™ *UK Ltd.*
500 Avebury Boulevard
Central Milton Keynes, MK9 2BE
www.authorhouse.co.uk
Phone: 08001974150

© *2007 Bud & Gertrude Hitt. All rights reserved.*

No part of this book may be reproduced, stored in a retrieval system, or transmitted by any means without the written permission of the author.

First published by AuthorHouse 2/19/2007

ISBN: 978-1-4259-7733-7 (sc)

Printed in the United States of America
Bloomington, Indiana

This book is printed on acid-free paper.

Contents

Foreword — vii

Introduction — ix

1. Sickness Be Gone! — 1
2. Turn Around! — 3
3. A Holy Spirit Knee — 5
4. He Saw the Devil — 9
5. My Background — 13
6. The Wrong Room — 23
7. Our Daughter's Prayer — 29
8. Even a Car Can Use a Prayer — 33
9. Madelaine & Velma — 35
10. The Fuel Pump — 41
11. One In a Million — 45
12. God Heals Even Via TV — 51
13. Go To Lugbill's — 53
14. The Unlisted Number — 57
15. Gertrude's Death Row Experiences — 59
16. No Altar Call — 63
17. Glory Row! — 65
18. The Lump is Gone! — 75
19. He Gave it all to Jesus! — 77
20. Shopping in the Ladies' Department — 87
21. Two New Births and a Motorcycle — 91
22. She's in a Coma! — 93
23. The Unforgettable Trip — 97
24. Rest Home Experiences — 103
25. Sore Neck Healed — 107
26. Sixteen Inches From Heaven — 109
27. Hawaii — 113
28. My Correctional Experiences — 121

29. It Happened At Christian Retreat	129
30. In A Heartbeat	133
31. When Some Prayers Go Unanswered	135
32. Classmates	145
33. My Aching Back	147
34. Only Half a Kidney	149
35. Just One More Bite!	151
36. Who Opened the Door?	155
37. Goodbye Sun City	159
38. Only a Little Scar	165
39. Spurs, Be Gone!	167
40. Gertrude's Healings	169
41. We Can't Operate—Too Dangerous!	175
42. The Case of the Lost Camera	179
43. Be Ready!	183
44. Stay Away!	187
45. What Boils?	189
46. Respond to a Hurting World	191
47. For God So Loved The World	195
48. David's Healing	197
Friend's Poem	203

Foreword

 I have known of Bud and Gertrude Hitt's ministry for more than twenty years, but came to know them on a more personal level only a few years ago. I believe that day to have been orchestrated by God and consider it a privilege to now be more acquainted with them personally in such a special way. Though you haven't seen them on television or read about them in the national press, I believe that they are two of God's most highly esteemed servants over the past fifty years, though they will humbly claim that they have been nothing more than obedient servants—which indeed they have been.
 This book contains numerous stories of some of their ministry-related experiences over the years. Though the stories themselves were first written down by Bud and then transcribed by Gertrude before being passed to me, it has been my privilege to initially compile their stories into book format. Many times I literally wept to read how God answered prayer in such miraculous ways. My personal prayer for the reader is that these stories will touch your heart as they did mine.
 The intent of this book is for believers to know that God uses "ordinary people" who, in obedience, will merely put their faith and trust in Him, and in the unfailing promises of His Word. May this book be a blessing to you as you read this wonderful collection of ministry experiences they have had over the years. May it also serve to increase your faith in the One and only God who empowers ordinary men and

women with such wonderful gifts, and who always honors a childlike prayer of faith. May God receive all the Glory for this work.

David Rand
Archbold, OH

Introduction

    This book is a collection of stories representing actual events that my wife and I have experienced over the past forty years.

    During those years, we have had the privilege of being blessed by our Lord on so many memorable occasions. As I would relate those experiences to others over the years, I was often encouraged to write them in a book. This happened so many times that I began to keep notes on some of our experiences and my wife would then type them up, which notes have now yellowed with age. As I recently felt led to get them out and review them, I began to feel impressed that now was the time for them to be compiled into a book.

    One evening after a bible study at Judy and David Rand's home, I related this to David and he offered to edit and compile our book. I was excited at the potential of all this and started scribbling down other experiences that the Lord seemed to allow me to vividly relive. Since English and spelling were not my best subjects in school, over the years Gertrude became an expert deciphering my scribbling and ramblings and spent many hours reviewing, verifying, retyping, adding, deleting, and looking up scriptures. Every Sunday afternoon, and many evenings late into the night, you would find her transcribing them to forward to David via her computer for further editing. We are blessed to have such a friend. We pray that you will be blessed and encouraged in the faith as you read each story.

We started in the restaurant business in 1948 in the small northwest Ohio town of Stryker, and in 1950 moved our equipment seven miles to our hometown of Archbold. In 1957 we started manufacturing and marketing custom-made archery bows, and in 1958 added trophies and awards to our line of products. In addition to operating our business at that time, from 1964-1977 our family traveled the tri-state area giving Gospel music concerts on weekends and evenings, at which we always presented the plan of salvation. In addition to those travels, we did many service club presentations, as well as a number of Christmas programs. The schedule was hectic at times because everyone in the family worked full-time at our business, but also traveled evenings and weekends to give Gospel concerts.

As our two oldest daughters married and grandchildren began arriving, that somewhat curtailed our singing and traveling, at least as a family, but my wife and I continued ministering on our own with her singing and me preaching and teaching. The two of us also began to do some team-teaching on the subject of evangelism, which is a subject dear to our hearts. In more recent years, we have concentrated most of our ministry efforts nearer to our home in northwest Ohio, serving in several churches and participating in a counseling/witnessing program via a local prison ministry evangelism outreach. Toward the end of 1993 we made the decision to retire and at that point sold our trophy business to a family member. Their website can be viewed at www.hittrophy.com.

During the years, God has used us for His Kingdom in rather simple, every-day-kinds of situations. We simply wish to relate some of those experiences as examples of what God has done because of His grace and love for ordinary people who obey Him. May these stories encourage you and lift your faith to know that you, too, can be used by God.

Bud & Gertrude Hitt
Archbold, Ohio 43502

Chapter 1
"Sickness Be Gone!"

We were on Interstate 75 heading home to Ohio after spending two-and-a-half months in Florida at a place called Christian Retreat. We had talked to my sister and found out that an uncle of ours was in The Toledo Hospital with a problem that had something to do with sores. Since we were headed back north, we thought that we would go by way of Toledo to visit uncle Gale at the hospital, who had remarried after his first wife died. After we walked into his room and exchanged greetings, his wife said to us,

"Just look at his face!"

We looked and he had blister-like sores all over his face, neck, shoulders, and even on his back.

I said, "What is this?"

She said that the doctors weren't quite sure what it was. I had talked to my uncle before about Jesus and he had made a profession of faith. I'm not sure how well he lived it, but nevertheless he did make a faith commitment. So we talked with him a while and said,

"Uncle Gale, we've come here to pray for you. We are on our way home and wanted to stop by and have a prayer with you."

We laid hands on him and said,

"In the name of Jesus, you sores, or whatever you are, loose him and get out of here—go!"

Now our prayer wasn't very long because we usually pray prayers that are right to the point. The Bible says that God already knows our needs and is just waiting for us to ask, exactly as Jesus told us to do in John 15:7. That is basically what we prayed, and only for about a minute, after which we left.

The next day, toward evening, we received a call from uncle's wife and she said,

"We're home!"

I said,

"You're home?"

She replied,

"Yes, we're home. Your uncle doesn't have a sore on his face, or anywhere! They're gone, totally and completely! This morning they were gone, so the doctor told us to go home.

I said,

"I've got to see this."

Now I know that we ask for things in faith, but when it happens we sometimes say, "I've got to see this!" So my wife and I went to Bryan to see uncle Gale. When we got there, we looked at him and he did not have a sore of any kind! God had completely wiped them away.

Chapter 2
"Turn Around!"

It was about 8:00 AM one morning when I was out front in the showroom where people came in to look at our trophies and awards. It's very rare that I was even out front because I usually was in the back working at my drawing board and doing artwork. In fact, I don't think I had been in my office more than a 'month of days' out of the forty years I was in business because I'm just not the type of person to sit still for very long. I had someone to handle the office part of the business, and my wife Gertrude took care of the financial end, so I never had to pay attention to any of those things. But one of those rare mornings when I was out front, in walks this man who said that he would like to speak to the boss. Now here I am in my jeans and work clothes, but I said,

"I'm the fellow you want to see."

He looked at me a little funny, but then said that he was from the Small Business Administration (SBA) and, because this was part of his territory, he just wanted to talk to me about the SBA. I had a plaque on the wall and so I pointed to it and said that I already belonged to that organization, as a friend of mine had signed me up years ago. Nevertheless, I invited him to sit down to talk. As you might guess, after a few minutes I was talking to him about the Lord. He told me that he was from Michigan and then began to tell me about his life. One thing led to another and, within a few minutes, he committed his life to the Lord Jesus Christ.

He said,

"You know, this is very strange that I'm even here right now."

He went on to tell me that he had driven all the way uptown to where the tree line starts (which was about a mile from my business) and at that point he seemed to hear a voice say,

"Turn around and go back to the business you just passed on the right hand side on the corner."

Though he was startled at such a voice, he thought he had better do that, and so he came back.

He continued,

"When I came in, you were here and this is what happened. That voice told me to come back here and now I know why!"

This man was so excited about all this that he said,

"I just have to go home and tell my wife what happened!"

You see, being obedient to the Lord can make all the difference. Did it just so happen that I was out front in the showroom when I usually wasn't in that area? No—I believe I was there because God wanted me to be there. That was a meeting that needed to take place in God's calendar, so God put things in place for it to happen. He placed me there and told this man to turn around and come back so that he could come to know the Lord Jesus Christ. What a Mighty God we serve!

Chapter 3
"A Holy Spirit Knee"

A number of years ago my wife purchased a moped (motor bike) for my birthday. I had such a great time pedaling this bike and taking it for long relaxing rides that I thought maybe something bigger would be even better, so I started looking for a small motorcycle. My son-in-law happened to have a motorcycle at the time, so he finally found one for me. Another year when I came back from Florida, he had found one just a little bigger, so I graduated upward. One year he found a real nice one for me up at Blissfield, Michigan, which is about 55 miles north of our place of business. As it happened, one of our good customers was also located in that town, so one day I called to make an appointment to see the motorcycle. The next day, Gertrude and I were on our way to Blissfield. We were greeted by a couple that was about our age who told us the motorcycle belonged to their son who had left it for them to sell because he had moved.

From this point I will refer to them as Mr. and Mrs. X to protect their privacy, though I'm sure they have told this story many times. Mr. X took me to see the motorcycle in his garage and, after looking it over, I bought it and told him that I would come back the next day to pick it up. Now the exciting part begins! When we went back into the house, Gertrude told me that Mrs. X had been watching the *700 Club*. She liked the daily prayer times they had on the *700 Club* because she had a knee that had only "half the parts," which required her to use crutches as her only means of walking. We told her that we would like to pray for her, but first we wanted to talk to them about Jesus. After a few minutes they both gave their hearts to the Lord. As we were talking, Mr. X went into the other room and came back with a Christian book that their son had given them, at which point we were quite certain that their son was a believer. While we do believe in doctors, we also believe that we first should ask God for our needs and then trust Him for the right answer. Jesus said in John 14:12, "I tell you the truth, anyone who has faith in me will do what I do." So we were just doing what Jesus said we were to do; namely, praying for a hurting person. Mrs. X told us that she had been going to a medical clinic in Toledo and, up to that point, they hadn't been able to help her. I can still see Gertrude and I getting down on our knees and praying that God would in some miraculous way heal Mrs. X's knee. After we prayed, we left, and the next day, as I had promised, I went back and brought the motorcycle back to Archbold.

About three weeks passed when I received a telephone call from Mrs. X at our place of business.

"Mr. Hitt," she said, "This is Mrs. X—do you remember me?"

I couldn't help but chuckle as I said,

"How could I ever forget your unusual name?" and she, too, started to laugh.

"Mr. Hitt," she said, "I'm not using crutches anymore; in fact, I don't even use a cane. I am completely healed! The doctors at the clinic showed me the x-rays that still confirm that half my knee joint is gone and told me, 'Mrs. X, you can't be walking,' but, Mr. Hitt, I am!"

[While the doctors couldn't understand how she could possibly be walking with only "half a knee," I knew that God had put in what I call "Holy Spirit parts" that even x-rays couldn't detect.] After praising the Lord for a few minutes, we hung up and I thought that was the end of the story, but God had more.

As summer is a very hectic season at our trophy business, all that work kept me busy delivering orders. When I received an order for Blissfield, Michigan, I delivered the trophies myself and then went to see Mr. and Mrs. X, but they weren't home that day; however, I knew that God would have another time. Later that summer, my wife and I, along with our daughter and her husband, decided to go to the *Hathaway*

House, which is a large plantation-type house at Blissfield, Michigan that had been turned into a restaurant. Because the three of them are crab-leg fans, when I grew weary of watching them trying to get little bites here and there, I excused myself and found a phone booth to call Mr. and Mrs. X. Mrs. X answered and I said,

"This is Bud Hitt. We're here in town and I thought I would give you a call to see if we could come over to see you."

She could hardly believe her ears as she said that she had been looking all day for our telephone number because she wanted to talk to us. (God put us right there on His timetable.) I went back to the table and told everyone that we were going to see Mr. and Mrs. X and that she had been trying to find our phone number.

After entering their home and introducing our family, our son-in-law said,

"My father-in-law has told me many stories of God's healing power, but you are the first ones that I have had the privilege to meet."

We could see that she was walking normally as she began to tell us about a recent trauma she had had. She said that she started having a heart attack and that Mr. X called the rescue squad, which took her to a Toledo hospital. She said that she kept saying all the way to the hospital,

"In Jesus Name, I am being healed."

After many tests there at the hospital, the doctors all agreed that she indeed was healed. Although they had been church members before we met them that in itself did not make them true believers in the Lord. However, after her miraculous healings, she learned how to really praise the Lord and what it meant to be a believer in Christ.

40th Wedding Anniversary; Gertrude & Bud Hitt with daughters Candy, Penny, Dawn

Chapter 4
"He Saw the Devil"

Ed, who was one of the salesmen that called at our place of business, became a good friend over the years and we would often get together with him and his wife. During this time, since our family was still giving music/ministry programs, and because Ed was in charge of the entertainment for the *Lions Club* banquet, he asked us to come and give the program. So we did and, as always, finished by telling them how they could know Jesus Christ. Ed later told me that everyone was talking about what they had heard and that when the bar was opened afterwards, no one wanted to drink any alcoholic beverages.

Several days later I had to deliver trophies to a city about 90 miles from us. When I was on my way back, I heard this quiet voice say,

"Go to Ed's home."

I knew that I was within five miles of his home but I also knew that it had been only two days since we had seen him and his wife at the *Lions Club* banquet. However, I suddenly found myself turning left off the busy highway, not giving a thought to check the oncoming traffic. I realized immediately what I had done and pulled the car to a stop and looked back to see if I had foolishly crossed in front of any traffic. To my relief and surprise, not a car or truck was in sight from either direction. As I continued on to Ed's home, I said,

"Lord you must have something really special for this visit!"

When I arrived at Ed's home, his wife answered the door and invited me to come in and eat with them. Ed wasn't home yet, but seated at the table were their three children and a lady that she introduced as Maria. I thanked her for the dinner invitation, but said that I had only stopped for a few minutes because I felt compelled to tell them about something that Jesus had done for me recently. As I related that story, their 14-year-old son started to cry. I walked up to the table and said to him,

"You want to know Jesus, don't you?"

He answered,

"Yes."

So I took him into the living room where we got down on our knees and he proceeded to ask Jesus into his life. When we went into the kitchen, he told them what had happened—that he had just asked Jesus to come into his life. As we were talking, Maria asked if we could talk privately, so Mrs. Ed, Maria, and I went into the living room. Maria wanted me to pray for her husband that he would get closer to God. I said,

"Let's get down on our knees and talk to the Lord, but before we pray for your husband I have something to ask you; "If you were to die right now, do you know for sure that you would go to Heaven?"

She replied that she did not. Then I continued,

"Would you like to know for sure?"

She said

"Yes!"

I introduced her to Jesus and then prayed for her husband that he would draw closer to the Lord. She told me no more about her husband than that he needed prayer. After praising the Lord for her salvation, I headed back home rejoicing at what God had done by sending me to Ed's home, once again thinking that was all there was to it. However, the next day I received a call from Ed's wife who very excitedly told me that Maria had just called her minutes before and related the following addition to the story.

Mrs. Ed said that Maria's husband was a doctor and that he had gone to Cincinnati for a medical convention and had taken his office nurse with him. Early the next morning Maria's husband returned extremely upset, crying out loudly,

"Maria, Maria, the Devil was in my room last night. I've got to find God! I've got to find God!"

It seems that when he looked at his nurse there in the motel room with him, she appeared to him like the Devil. He was so scared that he rushed out of the motel, got into his car, and drove the three-and-a-half hours home to tell Maria that he had to find God. He insisted that they go to see their priest right away, so they went and talked to the priest who told them to go to the altar and pray. After praying, he suddenly realized that he needed to go back to Cincinnati to pick up his suitcase and his nurse, whom he, in his frightened state of mind, had left behind. Some time later, Gertrude and I were invited to Ed's home for dinner with them and to meet Maria's husband. After dinner, he became very nervous and said that he had to leave for an appointment, exiting in such a hurry that we never had the chance to talk to him about Jesus. The last we heard, Maria and her husband had gone overseas for further medical training.

Early years of " The Gospel Hits" L-R; June Metcalf, Pianist Candy, Penny, Bud, Gertrude, Dawn

Postscript:

This past summer we had a surprise visit from Mr. and Mrs. Ed, who had long ago moved to Florida. Their children are now grown and their fourteen-year-old son in this story now has a grown daughter who just happened to call them on their cell phone while they were at our house. Mrs. Ed excitedly told her that they were visiting in Ohio at the home of the man who had led her father to the Lord when he was fourteen. We later asked about Maria, but they sadly told us that she and her husband had divorced. Maria moved to another state and went into business for herself. One day someone came in to the store and murdered her and her office girl. We were happy to know that Maria had come to know the Lord personally before that tragic event took her life.

Early days of "Gospel Hits"
Gertrude, Candy, Dawn, Penny, & Bud

Chapter 5
"My Background"

You know, my life hasn't always been like this, though. I wasn't even raised in a Christian home. When I was three years old, my folks moved from a farm near Bryan, Ohio, and came to Archbold. My dad got a job working for a bakery in Archbold, where I currently live, though that bakery has been gone for many years. He delivered bread and all kinds of baked goods to little stores in neighboring country towns because, in those days of course, there weren't such things as supermarkets—there were only little country stores. Dad would go from store to store, day after day, and was evidently making a living at it without any problem. The next thing I remember was one year later, in 1929, when I was four years old—it was called the Great Depression. To this very day, even though I was only four years old, I can still see in my mind's eye my mom and dad standing there by the kitchen door, holding each other and crying. As a little boy I remember wondering,

"Why are mommy and daddy crying?"

I was probably trying to figure out in my little mind why they were crying because I had never seen them cry before. I later came to realize it was related to the severity of the Depression and that my dad had lost his job. My folks weren't very old; my mom was only 22 years old and my dad was 26, so they were basically two young people. This is the life I can remember, and how we all lived through the days of the Depression.

I guess I didn't know that we were poor because everyone else was poor also.

Mom and Dad made it through the hard times as Dad found a job at a factory in Archbold that hired some people during the Depression. I don't know what my dad did to keep us going, but he managed. It was at that time that I learned how to make things with my hands and I suppose that's how I became a woodworker, because my Dad ended up doing some woodworking labor for other people and then began his own woodworking business in later years. As I was growing up, we never went to church. I suppose I went to Sunday School four or five times during my youth and teen years, as occasionally different ones would ask if I wanted to go, and, whenever they did, I would go.

We didn't even have a Bible in our home, but my folks were still good people and everyone liked them. They probably were about as "good as they come" and lived a good life, but as time went on I desired even less to go to Church or Sunday School. That was in the days when a preacher came into our public school on Good Fridays and other religious holidays to give sacred programs. We would have what was called an "assembly" and you would go and listen to the preacher talk and people sing. That was before they decided to take God out of the schools and make schools better—better all right, as in <u>not</u>. Things have just gone downhill since. But nevertheless, this is the way it went. I believed in God, and in Heaven and Hell, and I believed that Jesus Christ was the Son of God and that He came here to earth. I believed in Christmas and believed that Jesus was born on Christmas Day. I believed that He was nailed to a cross, rose from the dead, and went back to Heaven where He was seated at the right hand of God—but just 'believing' all that didn't make me a Christian.

I never dated, or even had the desire to date, until I was sixteen. I just liked to play basketball and run track because I liked sports. Going into my junior year, a buddy and I participated in the Junior Play. He was from the farm and had an automobile that he could drive and come in to town to the high school to practice at night. We started dating a couple of the girls who were also in the play. This went on for a time and I ended up dating several different girls. I started running around as a teenager and got into a little drinking now and then, but was never into big trouble. My buddies and I had a place to go where someone would

Power In Ordinary People

buy the drinks for us. During the summer of 1942, between my junior and senior years, I was helping a friend on the roof of an old farmhouse and slid off, ending up in the hospital pretty-badly damaged. I had a couple of broken bones and some back injuries, but didn't know how adversely that fall would impact my life until a year later.

During high school, I was taking flying-related courses that were being given during those World War II years because I wanted to become a fighter pilot or fly a bomber in the army. When I graduated from high school and took my physical, I was rejected. It was then I realized that the damage I had sustained from that fall was going to keep me out of the military. Yet, one by one, all my buddies passed their exams and left for active service. It was about that time my sister and brother-in-law moved to Ypsilanti, Michigan to work in the bomber plant there that made B-24s. My sister asked if I would like to come up and stay with them and work in the bomber plant. Since I also had an aunt and uncle in that area, and with my dream (though fading fast) to fly bombers, I decided in the winter of 1943-44 that I would make the move to Ypsilanti to earn a little money.

Even with family there, I'd still come back to Archbold almost every weekend. I always had plenty of gas because I had friends that were farmers, so even when gas became rationed they were able to get me gas tickets. Then, in the spring of 1944, my best friend from Archbold was finally drafted. That's an important part of this story. Since his dad was the Postmaster, and because his son (my buddy) would have to give up his mail route to go into the service, that set of circumstances created a job opening for me back in my hometown. After checking with my buddy's dad (the Postmaster), I decided that I would move back to Archbold and become a mailman.

By this time all the guys from Archbold were gone, and I was the only fellow left around town. While I admit that I was somewhat disappointed about being rejected for military service, the underlying advantage was that I had all the girls in town. They liked to go up to the lake, and this was in the Big Band days. We would go to Hamilton Lake or Manitou Beach where there was a big dance floor and where the Dorsey's and many of the Big Bands of that era would play. I would take the girls there, and of course would always be going steady with one of them. [I once tried "two at a time," but that didn't work out so well.] Nevertheless,

I had seen this one girl at *LaChoy Chinese Foods* in Archbold. When we were in school, my buddy (the one who got drafted) and I worked at *Lachoy's* one summer and we saw her there. I remarked to him how cute she was and that I'd sure like to go with her, to which he replied, "No—you don't want to go with her."

After I moved back from Ypsilanti, I carried the mail all winter. That was a really cold winter from around the first of December to the first of April, but finally spring came. As I was delivering mail to Archbold area businesses, I spotted this little *LaChoy* girl sitting in a car, so I stopped to talk with her. We talked and talked and talked, and would you believe that I held up the United States mail for about an hour and a half trying to get a date with her, yet all the time wondering, "Why?" [I thought, I've got all the girls already, so why in the world would I want a date with this one?] But she was awfully cute and finally said "yes" (maybe that was the challenge for me). I found out later that the reason she hesitated so long was because she had heard rumors about me being kind of on the wild side, which was somewhat true, but she didn't really know that for sure at the time. She finally decided that she would go out with me—just once.

I went to pick her up for our first date, but the funny thing about this 'first date' was that, on my way out to her house, I forgot her name! I had graduated with her sister, who was two years older than she was, but the little *LaChoy* girl I wanted to date was two years younger than me, which in my day meant that I "didn't even know she was in school." I mean, in our little school a 'big senior' wouldn't bother to get to know a 'little sophomore,' so I didn't. I thought that if her mom or dad answered the door, my "way out" was to just ask for her sister when I got there, whom I did know. But, as it turned out, it wasn't her mom or dad, or even her sister, who answered the door—it was my little *LaChoy* girl. [Later that evening, I admitted to her that I had forgotten her first name and so she kindly reminded me her name was Gertrude.] We got in the car and started down the road, heading to a little town to go to the theatre there. In those days you didn't have to worry about theater shows being violent, or out of line, or sexually immoral—they were just good ol' shows back then. We weren't down the road more than six or seven miles when she said to me,

"What does God mean in your life?"

I immediately thought,

"Man, what do I have here? This is something else if she's going to start talking about God!"

We went to the show and before the night was over I knew that this was the girl that I wanted to be my wife. I just knew it! We kept going together and she kept talking to me about the Lord and explaining things because I had never read anything in the Bible since we didn't even have one at home. I always said, with tongue in cheek, that Matthew, Mark, Luke, and John could have been a quartet singing down in Toledo because I honestly didn't know anything about the Bible. Eventually, it finally got through to me that Jesus Christ died for me, and, that when he died on the cross and shed his precious, holy blood, it was to wash away my sins. I finally became a Christian thanks to my little *LaChoy* girl, Gertrude. Sixteen months later we were married, and since our marriage in 1946 we're still going strong and doing things together. I wanted to share all this with you so that you would know that God can change anyone.

About a year and a half after we were married, we were both working in Stryker, another small town close to Archbold. [Since my wife didn't drive at that time, we both got a job in the same town.] She worked in an office and I worked at a finishing job where they manufactured mobile homes. We'd meet every day uptown at a restaurant that was run by an old bachelor who put out a pretty good meal. He kept asking us, "Why don't you kids buy this (restaurant)?" But we didn't have any money to buy anything. So after several months, he came up with a proposal that he would lease the restaurant to us for a certain amount of money. He put a price on the place and said that, at the end of the year, if we decided that we wanted to buy it, he would deduct the year's lease payments we had made and apply that amount to the purchase price. Nearing the end of operating the restaurant for that year, we decided, "Why not purchase it?" We went to a local bank to apply for a loan even though everyone told us that we wouldn't get the money. When we got a call from the bank and they told us that they were going to lend us the money, we were very surprised. What we didn't know until later was that the Chairman of the Board was a farmer and that he often came to eat at our restaurant. To my good fortune, it turned out that he also knew my father-in-law, who was an honest farmer who threshed for many of the other farmers in that area. Since he knew my father-in-law's good reputation, and also knew and observed that Gertrude and I worked very hard at the restaurant (and that she was a great cook!), he said that his bank would loan us the money. That's how we got into the restaurant business, and we stayed in Stryker for the next two-and-a-half years. In 1950 our first daughter was born and, while my wife was still in the hospital, I decided that we would sell the building and go back to Archbold and put in a drive-in restaurant, which is exactly what we did. We went a mile out in the country and, at the corner of a pasture field, put in a drive-in restaurant that became very successful. We were very busy with all that—more work than anyone could imagine. Some days we found ourselves working as many as twenty hours.

One night some fellows came in and wanted me to go deer hunting with them. As I was a gun hunter, I said that deer season wasn't in right now, but they told me that they were going bow and arrow hunting. [I was also building a house in addition to running the restaurant. I built it myself, putting up every rafter and everything else with only hand tools at that time. I had it all enclosed with cedar siding, though I didn't have the walls finished on the inside yet.] I got to thinking the next day that my uncle had a bow, so why not run over to Stryker and ask him if I can use it to go deer hunting with these guys? He loaned me an old lemonwood bow, but when the guys came back later that evening and asked if I was going hunting with them, I told them, "No, you couldn't hit anything with one of those things!" I explained that I had shot that bow in the afternoon at a box inside my unfinished house and had put a hole in the wall! They took me outside under the lights and showed me that I could learn to shoot it right, and I ended up going bow and arrow hunting with them. It made such a lasting impression on me that when I came back from that hunting experience, the next thing I did was to start making archery bows.

They were starting to make laminated bows in the early 1950's and soon I had designed and manufactured some rather nice bows. My wife also started getting a little interested in archery, and soon our employees and workers wanted to buy bows. Shortly after that, a fellow came in and said that he was going to start a sporting goods store in a neighboring town and wanted to know if I would make some bows for him. With that much of a demand for bows, we decided that maybe other people would want them too, so we bought an adjoining piece of land, put up a small building, and started making bows and other related archery equipment. My wife got so good handling a bow that she won 11 State championships (Ohio) and, in 1961, an International Indoor championship at Fort Wayne, Indiana. As she got better and better, in 1963 we flew out to California for her to compete. Though she shot well at that competition, the point I wish to make is that on July 29, 1963, as we were flying back from that competition to Chicago, I looked out the window and said rather longingly, "Lord, there's got to be more to this Christian life." I was nervous, by the way, and made some vows to the Lord that I might not have made had I not been so nervous. You see, I was a little anxious because I had flown in propeller planes before and they didn't behave like this one did—this one would shake and the wings would go up and down, and I thought, "Boy, I'm not too sure about this thing."

Nevertheless, I had been thinking for a long time that there's just got to be more to this Christian life, and this happened seventeen years after I had gotten saved. As I looked out the airplane window, I said,

"Lord, I'll do anything you want. I'll take my family, we'll live in a tent, and we'll live in Africa" (that's where missionaries always seemed to go, at least the ones that came and talked at our church).

We always went to church and Sunday School; all these years we never failed to do such things as that. We were very faithful, but I knew that there was something else that I was missing. So I just totally poured out my heart to the Lord and told Him that I was willing to do anything, to go anywhere—it didn't make any difference. When I turned back from that prayer and looked around that plane, for the first time I began to see lost people just as if scales had fallen off my eyes. We flew into Chicago and got home later that night, and the next morning I was up early reading the Bible. I started reading the Bible every day for the next year, day in and day out, for one to two hours every morning—reading and reading. I was so hungry to read and learn as much as I could, that I just read and read. One morning as I was sitting at the table reading the Bible, I came to the verse that talks about "going to the uttermost parts of the world and preaching the gospel" when I heard a voice. I'm sure no one else would have heard it had they been there, but it was just as plain as if someone was speaking to me. It said

"Bud, if you were in Africa this morning, where would the uttermost parts of the world be?"

Now, I don't know if I said this out loud or not, but I said/thought--
"Lord, it could be anywhere—even right here."
"Then why don't you get busy?" He said.

You see, if I were in Africa this morning, the uttermost parts of the world could be right here where I am now. At that moment, I knew I was to stay in our little town, run our business, and that God was going to open up doors for me that I couldn't even imagine.

Shortly after that, one Sunday night at our church they made a call for people to go out to local migrant camps. On the way home, and I don't recall which one of us said it first, but one of us said,

"I've got to go to those camps."

Then the other one said,

"That's what I was going to say!"

We took our girls and started to minister and sing at local migrant camps with other people. My wife and our two oldest daughters sang as a trio in the car as we traveled around northwest Ohio for my wife to compete at archery shoots. We would always take our girls with us, especially during the summertime because they were out of school. As they got a little older, at 13 and 16, we were asked to go along with a migrant minister to churches to recruit more help for the migrant camp ministry. The girls would sing and I would give a testimony, and that's how our ministry started. The girls got so good at singing and blended so well that for the next thirteen years we traveled and did concerts most weekends, and even some evenings during the week. We tried to stay within 100 miles of our home, as we still needed to work at our archery business. We certainly weren't in that ministry for the money, but were doing it simply to present the Good News of Jesus Christ. I would present the Gospel at every service and let the people know how they could be born again. As another side bit of information, our family ended up making two record albums in Nashville.

During those days of going into the migrant camps, one time we went to a rather large camp. That night, there were about 50 migrants gathered around sitting on tomato hampers. We were in a big circle, but about half of them couldn't speak English—only Spanish. I asked one young lady there, who was about 20 years old, if she would interpret for me because she could speak English quite well. She agreed, so I talked with them for a while, told them about Jesus, and how they could ask Christ into their lives and be born again, with the young girl interpreting everything into Spanish. When I was finished, I asked for those who would like to have Christ come into their lives to stand up. The whole bunch stood up! I thought, surely they didn't understand what I meant, so I asked them all to sit back down. I told the interpreter that she and I were going to go to the Spanish-speaking migrants and make sure that they understood why they were being asked to stand up. My wife and others went down the other side to do the same for those who understood English. When we finished making certain that they all understood what we were going to be asking, we asked a second time if they wanted Jesus to come into their lives and they all stood up again! Since this was clearly a "God thing," we had them pray a prayer to ask Jesus to come into their lives.

When I was finished, I said to the young lady who was interpreting for me,

"How about you?"

She said,

"Yes, I meant it, too!"

At this same meeting, there were five boys standing in the back who mocked us nearly the whole time. I tried to get them to come over, but they wouldn't come, so when we got ready to leave, I said,

"Fellows, I'd like to talk to you about this."

Because they didn't want to do that, I asked them if they would just let me pray for them. They said, okay. My prayer went something like this—

"Lord, if there is any way that you could give some kind of a sign to these fellows that you are really real, I ask you to do that."

What I'm about to tell you, I've never seen anything like it before, and I don't know if I'll ever see anything like it again, but it's absolutely true. All of a sudden, when I finished praying that prayer, as we were all standing there, it seemed like a falling star whizzed right over our heads and landed in the woods! Though we thought it must have been higher in the air than what we perceived it to be, it seemed to come right over the top of our heads. The five boys screamed and everyone yelled, but all five boys received Jesus Christ into their lives that night! Now, that was a rather unusual thing, but God is indeed an unusual God. In fact, God is a *supernatural* God who does *supernatural* things. This is only one of the many stories during our years of migrant camp ministry.

We stayed in the migrant ministry until certain government regulations forced tomato farmers to erect better housing, almost like motel accommodations. Because most small farmers couldn't afford to do that, they quit raising tomatoes, all of which led to the closing of many migrant camps. Later on, when they developed more sophisticated mechanical techniques for harvesting tomatoes, that added all the more to the closing of many migrant camps, though there are still a few of them in existence in our area.

My Little "LaChoy" girl.

Chapter 6
"The Wrong Room"

I hurriedly stepped off the elevator at St. Vincent's Hospital in Toledo and walked into the room. I was shocked to find a lady in her fifties lying in the bed instead of our friend, Carol.

"Where's Carol?" I asked.

I stood there in bewilderment looking around the room wondering what had happened to Carol.

I had needed some parts for a machine I was building at our shop, so I went to Toledo to get them. As I was driving the 45 miles, I kept wondering what exciting thing God had in mind for me that day. Those years had been so exhilarating since Jesus was on the throne of my life, so much so that each day I looked forward to a new experience from the Lord. I bought my supplies and nothing unusual happened, not even a chance to witness. As I left the last place, the Holy Spirit seemed to lead me to go to St. Vincent's Hospital to visit Carol. That seemed rather strange, as Gertrude and I had just visited her three days before. Carol, a lovely young schoolteacher from our town, had become very ill on her honeymoon and became paralyzed from her neck down. Each chance we and other friends had, we would visit Carol and pray for her complete healing. We claimed God's promises and "stood in the gap" as we continued to believe God for her healing.

I parked my car in the hospital garage and wondered why I wasn't rushing back home to finish my job with the parts I had just bought. I stepped into the vacant elevator and pushed the button for the fifth floor. It was the middle of the afternoon and no one else got on the elevator. When it stopped, I stepped off, greeted one of the nurses, and quickly headed for Carol's room right next to the nurses' station. My surprise was quite evident to the three people in the room. I explained to them that Carol had been in this room for over six months and that we had just visited her three days ago. The lady politely responded,

"I don't understand how that could be, as I have been in this room for over ten days."

A young woman in her mid-twenties was sitting in a chair at the foot of the bed while the patient's husband sat in a chair over by the window. I was quite puzzled as all three of them began to verify the length of time that this lady had occupied this room.

"I can't understand this," I said, "Carol has been in room 534 for over six months."

Then they all answered in unison,

"You're not in room 534—you're in room 434."

I must have had a silly look on my face as I wondered how I had made such a mistake. But I knew that no one else was on the elevator and, since no one had gotten on, how did it stop at the fourth floor? My thoughts were racing.

"All right Lord, You pushed that button for a reason, so I better find out why. Since I'm here, I may as well visit awhile."

I introduced myself and told them that I was from Archbold, Ohio. The man responded that he had been born and raised in Bryan, a town only fifteen miles from where we lived. This opened up the conversation because I was born just outside of Bryan where most of my relatives still live. As we talked about Bryan, I found out that, as a boy, the man had known my grandfather and many of my uncles. Though I knew that God had directed me here for a reason, I still wasn't certain as to why, but I was just about to find out. The conversation turned to spiritual matters and, as I conversed with the mother in the bed, I learned that the girl sitting in the chair at the foot of the bed was their daughter and that she was a Christian. The mother quickly joined the conversation and said,

"I have been saved by Jesus, too."

The lady's husband, whom I will just call Dad, added that he was not saved, but without blinking an eye I continued talking to the daughter. She said that she attended the most wonderful church where Sunday School was interesting and the pastor preached the Gospel. All three of us were enjoying our conversation about the Lord and the daughter's church. I then learned that the mother's left leg had been amputated below the knee and that her right leg had the same kind of infection that led to the partial amputation of the other leg. I now knew for certain that God had sent me there to pray for the mother. I was about to tell them that I wanted to pray when the Lord impressed on me that I was to tell the daughter the name of her church denomination.

If you have ever had a spiritual conversation with the Lord, where He gives you special knowledge about something that would otherwise be unknown to you, and then directs you to reveal that to someone, you feel sort of strange because you know that the other people in the room didn't hear any voice, and yet you did. In fact, you may be as shook up as I was when I first received this gift [the *Word of Knowledge* referred to in I Corinthians 12:8]. You may question yourself, as I did, and think, "Is this the Lord or is it me?" I then blurted out,

"I know the denomination of your church."

Now I had committed myself!

"What if I'm wrong?" I thought.

Almost simultaneously the mother and daughter both cried out,

"What is it? Tell us!"

At that moment I seemed to lose faith in believing that God really told me to say this. Instead of answering them, I took the coward's way out and asked the mother if I could pray for her leg.

"Oh, yes, please do," she answered.

I was sure that I had found a "way out," so I laid my hands on her and started praying for the healing of her body and for the leg sores to dry up. As I was praying for her, that same inner voice said,

"Tell her what their denomination is."

Again, I argued,

"What if I'm wrong, Lord?"

At that instant I knew I had really implied, "Lord, what if <u>You</u> are wrong?" I knew immediately that I had to trust Him and just tell them what He told me to tell them. Without a moment's hesitation, I finished the prayer "In the name of Jesus," and then turned to the daughter and said,

"You go to a Methodist church."

They both exclaimed,

"How did you know? How did you know?"

All I could say was,

"The Lord revealed it to me and He told me to tell you that I knew."

I looked at "Dad" still sitting by the window and knew why I had to tell them—it was to have his 'eyes' opened to the fact that all of this was from God. At that point I walked back over to the daughter who had told me that her ankle was developing the same problem as her mother's leg, knelt down by her, and said,

"I want to pray for your ankle to be healed in the Name of Jesus."

She pleaded,

"Please do!"

After praying for her, I stood up, walked over to "Dad," sat in a chair next to him, took out the *Four Spiritual Laws* booklet, and said,

"Now I want to talk to you about Jesus."

With tear-filled eyes he muttered,

"I went to Sunday School as a boy and I know the Bible."

As he said this, he was putting on his glasses ready to read and hear what God wanted me to tell him. When I finally left, room 434 was saturated with the joy and peace of Jesus. When I arrived at Carol's room, we praised the Lord together over what had just happened. All the way home I continued praising the Lord for the miraculous ways in which He works.

Carol Storrer signing books after she spoke and Gertrude sang. (See story of the Wrong Room.)

Postscript By Gertrude:

This story goes back to the late 70's, which began a five-year struggle for Carol to overcome this rare disease that had made her a quadriplegic. She almost died a couple of times. Through much encouragement and prayer she would get better, only to have relapses; however, her new husband, Tom, stood faithfully with her. Their son, Jeff, was born while she was still paralyzed, a true miracle baby. Carol became a Christian in the hospital and just clung to scriptures of healing. Our small town rallied and had a benefit supper for them. Many of us visited, encouraged, and prayed with her. When she came home, we were the volunteers. God opened the door for Carol to have plasma exchange treatments, which the doctors felt would do no good, but she now leads a normal life and is a blessing to many. A friend of Carol's wrote a book of her trials and triumphs called "Walking Home."

Carol has become like a daughter and is very dear to me. After her book came out, she was asked to speak about her healing in many churches, so for years I drove her to those services where she spoke and I sang. Having been a home economics teacher, Carol sews and cooks, as well as takes care of her home. I do not sew, so when I need something fixed I go to Carol. She also blesses me when my birthday rolls around with delicious piecrusts for my freezer. She has also been a blessing to our daughter Dawn who lives only two houses across from her.

It is very important for family and friends to visit, encourage, and pray for people when doctors give up. Sometimes God will lay someone upon your heart who is going through a tough time whom you really may not know all that well. That is what happened in Carol's case. Carol was amazed at the people who visited her that she did not know personally. Though she was our daughter Candy's teacher, we really didn't know her, yet what a wonderful friend she became to us. I would have missed knowing her had we not begun visiting her.

Carol Storrer & family.

Chapter 7
"Our Daughter's Prayer"

    In 1967, Gertrude was getting to the point where she didn't want to compete in archery anymore because our family was on the road singing so much, as many as ninety times a year, and we were still very busy in our archery business. Besides that, being a champion is not always easy, as some might think. They love you at first when you're a champion, but, and not meaning this in the wrong way, the ladies against whom Gertrude would compete knew that when she showed up they likely weren't going to win and Gertrude became very sensitive to that. So, she decided that she was going to get out of archery competition. However, for whatever reason, she decided that she wanted to go to *Cobo Hall* in Detroit and compete one last time in the International Indoor Championship. [Dawn, our oldest, would have been about 16; Penny, our second, about 13; and Candy Jo, about 3.] We left the three girls at home in the care of our secretary, and went to Detroit where Gertrude competed on a Saturday. We had also made arrangements with some Canadian friends of ours to go across the border and spend the evening with them, and go to church with them the next morning. They weren't really churchgoers, but, knowing that we were, they had made plans to get us to a church. So after Gertrude shot on Saturday, we went up to Canada to our friends. We got up the next morning and they took us to a church that they thought was of our denomination, which they supposed was the only church that we would attend. By afternoon, Gertrude wasn't sure if she wanted to go back to *Cobo Hall* and compete, but, as she had shot fairly well on Saturday, she decided to at least stop at *Cobo Hall* to see how the competition was going. [She shot well, but didn't take top honors that day, though that is not the point of this story; only that we were in Detroit and had to make the two-hour drive back home.] So around 6:00 PM, we decided it was time to start for Archbold.

We were on John Lodge freeway, which leads over to Route 94 past the Detroit airport. As we were heading out, I said,

"What am I doing on Ten Mile road? I can't be on Ten Mile road; I'm supposed to be on John Lodge freeway heading for 94."

Gertrude said,

"What's the difference?"

I said,

"I never left John Lodge freeway, so what am I doing on Ten Mile road? This has to be John Lodge freeway."

She said again,

"What's the difference? Let's just stop and get something to eat."

Now it was 1967, which is an important fact to the story. We stopped and went into a little restaurant. When the waitress came to take our order she said,

"How's the weather out there?"

I said,

"I don't know; it's a little cloudy. What do you mean?"

There was nothing wrong with the weather, as far as I knew. The waitress then proceeded to tell us that there were tornado warnings posted, and I said,

"There are?"

Just as I said that, all of sudden it started pouring and blowing, and were we glad we were inside! When we finished our meal, we got back into our car and drove down the highway. I said to Gertrude,

"Wow, look at that sign turned backwards! – Look at that car; it's sitting backwards in the ditch!"

I'll never forget that.

"What's going on?" I exclaimed.

I then remembered that the waitress had said there were tornado warnings, so I figured that there must have been a very strong wind that had come along there. It wasn't long until we saw some people helping another couple who had a little sports car that couldn't get through the high water under a viaduct. Since they had help, we continued on and finally reached home.

Our girls were there and we said that there must have been a tremendous storm that had taken place. Our oldest daughter, Dawn told us that June (our secretary) had dropped her off at our church that evening because Dawn wanted to be with her youth group, and then June took Candy and Penny over to her church. Dawn said that since she was the first one to the meeting, she was just sitting there waiting for the others to arrive when suddenly a cold chill seemed to come over her and a voice said,

"Your mom and your dad are in trouble."

She started praying and said,

"Oh God, I've never done this before, as I've never thought about mom and dad being in trouble because they travel so much, but wherever they are, just take care of mom and dad, please just take care of them."

I said,

"What time was that?"

She told us the time and I said,

"That's just about the time when we thought we were on John Lodge freeway but wound up on Ten Mile road. We don't even know how we got off John Lodge freeway."

As we tried to piece it all together, it had to be that God somehow took us from one place on the one road and put us in another place on another road, though we never had a sensation of any kind of physical movement. In my mind, as I've thought about this many times over the years, I have asked myself,

"Did I somehow turn off the highway?"

I honestly don't remember that I did, but our daughter's story brought chills when she told us that. We later found out that a line of tornados had come down across southern Michigan (1967) and wiped out many pavilions, trees, and cottages at Manitou Beach, and then came down across Route 23 and took out about five blocks of homes on the west side of Toledo. If our place on the road had been as we had initially planned after leaving *Cobo Hall*, we would have been right in the middle of that line of tornadoes. Instead, the Lord, in a miraculous answer to our daughter's prayer, somehow got us off the most dangerous road and placed us on Ten Mile road where we stopped to get something to eat and were out of the path of the most severe tornadic activity. He took care of us on that particular occasion in some miraculous way that we may never understand while on this earth. Isn't God good!

"Mom & Dad are in trouble."

Chapter 8
"Even a Car Can Use a Prayer"

Since I had developed a line of plaques for Christian bookstores, Gertrude and I took the motor home and headed south one year to call on Christian bookstores. At one gas stop, I was filling up the two tanks on our motor home. The second tank filled rather slowly because whoever installed it forgot to put in an air vent, so it took quite a while to fill. As I was waiting, I looked over and saw a car about 100 feet away with the hood up and a man saying to his wife,

"Try it again."

She'd try to start the car, but it just wouldn't turn over. He would then do something else under the hood, and she'd try again, but to no avail. I finally got my tank filled and when Gertrude went into pay, I walked over to the man and said,

"Got some problems?"

He said,

"Yes, this thing just won't start."

I said,

"You know what I'd probably do?"

He said,

"What?"

I said,

"I'd probably pray over it."

He said,

"What?!"

So I just laid my hands on the car and prayed,

"Father, in the name of Jesus, I ask You to start this car for them and just let it run good."

He looked at me rather funny, but said to his wife,

"Try it again."

She tried it and it started right up! He slammed the hood down, jumped in the car, closed the door, and took off and never said anything. He's probably wondering to this day how someone stopped and prayed for his car and the car actually started. Now I know that this isn't always the answer to things, that God would start your car in this way. But if He does, it may be that you better have it looked at later because who knows what God has in mind? I'm sure that this man, if he's still around today, will never forget what happened that day.

Chapter 9
"Madelaine & Velma"

Our youngest daughter, Candy, was enrolled at *Oral Roberts University* and we had just returned from taking her back in the Fall for her second year as a music performance major. Tom, our son-in-law, who is married to our oldest daughter, Dawn, told us that Madelaine, one of our valued long-time employees, was in the hospital in traction because of an old injury from an auto accident during her youth. As soon as we could, Gertrude and I headed to the hospital. When we walked into her room and greeted her, this was the first time I had seen anyone in traction with all those ropes and pulleys. She was glad to see us because the neurologist had told her that she had a ruptured disc, that half of another disc was also ruptured, and that she would need to have an operation. After visiting for a few minutes, I said,

"Madelaine, do you believe that Jesus can heal you?"

Without a moment's hesitation she responded emphatically,

"I know that He is going to heal me!"

Madelaine always looked so nice. When she came to work, she looked as if she was going someplace other than work. My wife and I have always appreciated her friendly, positive attitude—no matter how she felt. When she worked for us, I could be sure that she would always be interested in what I had to say about the latest thing that God had done, so I shouldn't have been surprised when she said,

"I know that He is going to heal me!"

We laid hands on her and, with all three of us in agreement, asked God to heal her in Jesus' name.

On the way home, we talked about her strong, positive faith evidenced by her believing that God was going to heal her back. The next day when the doctor came to check her over to make plans for an operation, Madelaine told him that she no longer had any pain and that the Lord had healed her. After Madelaine refused a less invasive operation, the doctor suggested that she take therapy. Madelaine told the therapist that she no longer had any pain and asked the therapist if she believed that God could heal people. The therapist replied that she did, so Madelaine told her that the Lord had healed her and she wouldn't need any therapy.

When Madelaine came home, different ones were surprised to see her walking uptown and would repeatedly say that they thought she was in the hospital. She told them that she had been, but that the Lord had healed her! She never hesitated to testify to the fact that God indeed had healed her. A couple of weeks after Madelaine's healing, her husband came home to find her piling up wood that he had cut for their wood burner. When he told her she shouldn't be doing that, she reminded him that the Lord had healed her and continued stacking the wood. About a year after her healing, one day at work she told me that the pain started to come back and she said that she very strongly said,

"Devil, the Lord has healed me and you're not going to bring that pain back!"

She said at that very instant it was gone and has never returned. In checking with her as to how long ago this was, she said that it was more than 20 years ago and, in my own way of confirmation, that would be correct because it was the year that Candy was starting her second year of college.

On a related story, Madelaine's sister-in-law, Velma, suffered with very painful arthritis and asked Madelaine if it would be all right for her (Velma) to come over to our house so that we could pray for her. I said to Madelaine,

"Why don't you pray for her? We aren't anyone special because it is God who does the healing. We only ask in the Name of Jesus."

Madelaine responded,

"No, she wants you to pray for her—and tonight if possible."

I called my wife and, since we were free that night, we had Velma come over for prayer. And once again, though there is nothing special about us, our great and awesome God answered our prayer and Velma said that the pain was gone.

About a month later, Velma called us from the hospital and asked us if we would come and pray for her husband Bill who was seriously ill at the time. When she told us that the doctor wasn't sure that Bill would make it through the night, we headed right to the hospital. I knew that Bill had been having some heart problems and already had a pacemaker, but that was all I knew. Velma met us in the lobby and told us the seriousness of his condition. We proceeded to Bill's room and talked with him, as he was still very alert. After visiting for about five minutes, I suddenly knew that I was to tell Velma to sit down and be quiet, but how do you tell someone you barely know to sit down and be still? I didn't want to tell her in a rude way, but I knew that I must say it because she was a person who was "blessed with the gift of speech." So, with great apprehension, I finally got the courage to interrupt her and said,

"Would you please sit down and not say anything. We want to talk to Bill."

I know that she was surprised when I said that, but she did sit down. Then I turned to Bill and said,

"You know that we came to pray for you, Bill, but first—If you were to die this very moment, do you know for sure that you would go to heaven?"

It may seem dumb to ask someone who might soon die that question, but God had lain upon my heart that this was the right moment to ask. Bill responded that he did not know, so I asked him if he wanted to know, to which he replied that he did. As Gertrude and I ministered to him, he cried and repented for about thirty minutes and asked Jesus into his heart. I think Gertrude and I both knew at that point that Velma would have probably answered for Bill if I hadn't asked her not to say anything. Receiving Christ as Savior is a personal thing and does not depend on your church membership or anything else, except the inner state of your own heart. Bill had to answer for himself, repent for himself, and ask Jesus into his life personally.

After we praised the Lord for his salvation, we then asked God to heal him. Once again, it was a rather short prayer, but to the point. The next morning when the doctor came in to examine Bill, he could not find anything wrong, other than his body was weak. He had received a healing sometime in the night. Velma made arrangements for him to go to a local rest home until his strength returned. He wasn't there long when Bill convinced Velma to take him home. We started going out to their home at least two times a week to visit and pray with them. At that time, Bill started watching every TV minister that he could and then when we would meet together, we would talk about what he had heard and share scriptures with him. Bill was a new creature in Christ, and as he became stronger he said that he would like to get on his tractor and help get the soybeans out of the field. We prayed with Bill and asked God to give him the strength to do that. A few nights later when we again went to disciple them, Bill wasn't there—he was out on the tractor! God gave him the desire of his heart. (Psalm 37:4.)

Bill and Velma would often call us at our winter home in Florida and we would pray with them over the phone. A few years later, while we were still wintering in Florida, Velma told us on the phone that Bill was very concerned about dying, so we told them that we would send someone from Ohio to share Scripture with him. When she called back a few days later, she said that our friend had shared scriptures about Heaven with Bill and that he was now completely at ease about dying. When we returned from Florida, we went to visit them and then went out to a fish fry together. Shortly after that, we received another call from Velma saying that Bill was in the local hospital once again with a large aneurysm just below his heart. Bill's spirits were low because the doctor had told him that, with his pacemaker and past heart problems, he wasn't sure that Bill could stand the seven-hour operation.

The doctor also told Bill's wife that, with or without the operation, Bill might die. Immediately we headed for the hospital and prayed that he would have peace, and then both of us prayed specifically for the surgeon who would be operating. In our prayer we asked that the doctor's hands would move in such a way that even he could not understand. We left the hospital not knowing that one hour later they would be transporting Bill to a Toledo hospital for the operation the next morning. After the operation, the surgeon came into the waiting room to speak with the family. He kept looking down at his hands and told them that the operation was a complete success, taking only a little more than an hour instead of the seven hours that he had anticipated. All these events took place within about a five-year period.

Sometime after Bill's operation, their 42-year-old son, Jerry, was in a Toledo hospital with cancer. As a friend of ours had his father in that same hospital, I decided that I would go along with our friend and visit Bill and Velma's son. As it turned out, their rooms were side by side. I went in to see Jerry and, as I greeted him, I could see by his face that things were not going well. He told me that the doctor had informed him that he had about a 20% chance of living another four months. I asked him if I could pray for him because the news that his doctor had was all bad and I wanted to talk to the only other doctor who could help him at this point—Jesus.

He said,

"I guess it can't hurt anything."

After praying for Jerry, I went to the room of my friend's father, visited for a few minutes, and had a prayer with him. Three days later I had to go to Toledo on business and, while there, decided to stop by and visit Jerry again. As I walked into his room and greeted him, he had a grim response.

"What's wrong?" I asked.

He replied that the news was even worse—his chances for survival had been revised downward to 5%. Where logic and reason end is where God can take over and show man that He is indeed God. I said to Jerry,

"Let's talk to Doctor Jesus again about this."

So we did, and after a short prayer I left. Soon after that, they sent him back home to gain strength for the cancer treatments. I visited him off and on for about three weeks until it was time for us to go to our winter home in Florida. After about two weeks in Florida, I was talking to our daughter Dawn when I asked her if she had heard anything about Jerry. She said,

"Dad, haven't you heard?"

"Heard what?" I replied.

She said that Jerry had gone in for a physical prior to starting the treatments and that they couldn't find any cancer in his body! This was approximately 18 years ago and it has not returned to this day.

We visited the family less frequently than before, as we began to give most of our free time to minister at the new correctional center (a five-county jail facility). About two years after Jerry's healing, Bill's body wore out and Velma took him to a convalescent home just over the line in Michigan, which was near their daughter's home. He was there only a short time when one day his young granddaughter came to visit him. After he had finished eating, she went over to the window to look outside. When she turned around to walk back over to grandpa, Bill was already in the arms of Jesus. He had slipped away with no pain or suffering, just as he desired. At his funeral, his pastor spoke of the change in Bill's life and the peace that he had. Another winter while we were in Florida, Velma also passed away. They were older than us and had lived full lives, and thus another chapter of friendship for us was closed.

We are still in contact with Madelaine even though she retired from *Hit Trophy*. Why God heals some and not others, I do not know, but we will continue to pray for people who need our prayers until we, too, go home to be in the arms of Jesus.

Chapter 10
"The Fuel Pump"

After a Bill Glass prison crusade at Leavenworth, Kansas, since we had our youngest daughter, Candy, with us, we decided to extend the trip into a vacation. So, we visited cousins in Colorado and then decided to go on to Spearfish, South Dakota, where the three of us enjoyed seeing the *Passion Play*. On the way back to Ohio, we weren't on the road very long before our vehicle started slowing down. The Interstate was very flat at that point, so it certainly wasn't the grade of the road. I kept trying to accelerate, but, the more I did, the more our motor home slowed down, until it finally seemed to level out @ 35 mph. As Gertrude was in the back, I told her that there was something wrong with the vehicle—it just wouldn't go any faster. She came up and sat bedside me and started praying for God to help us find someone who could help us. We had a 318 Dodge engine in this motor home, which was not a standard engine. There is nothing but miles and miles out there in South Dakota with very few ramps leading off to anywhere, let alone to full-service garages with mechanics. In a few minutes, as we were praying, an exit became visible. My wife said,

"There's one, there's one!"

I think she thought I must have been a dummy and just looked at me as I said,

"No, no, I'm not going to get off at that one," and I went right by.

She said,

"What are you doing? We need someone to help us and here the Lord provided a place to get off but you pass it by."

I said,

"I just don't think we're supposed to get off there."

She wasn't real happy about it and, to be honest, I was thinking to myself,

"That probably wasn't too smart."

We went on for at least another half hour before we saw another exit coming up, and this time I said,

"This is the one we're going to get off on."

We went up the ramp, came to the top, turned left and then right, and there was an old town right out of the Wild West with wide streets and old wooden buildings that looked just like one of those you would see in an old cowboy movie. I almost thought I was going to see Wild Bill Hickock come riding down the street; that's just the way it looked. Gertrude looked around and said,

"Where are we going to find any kind of a garage here?"

I agreed that it didn't look like much of a town, but I noticed a sign sticking out down the street a ways. The closer we got, the better we could see that it said, "Dodge trucks." I had a Dodge engine in this motor home, so I pulled up in front of the old building, went in, and there was an elderly man sitting in a rocking chair just swaying back and forth. He said,

"Can I help you?"

I said,

"I hope so. I have a motor home out here that I just can't get any speed out of; 35 mph is the best I can get."

He hollered at a young man, whom he said worked for him after school, and said that he would have him take a look at it. I could see there was someone else working back there; a mechanic, I presumed. When I saw the kid come out, I remember thinking to myself,

"He's going to give me this kid to work on it? Well, I guess that's the best I'm going to get."

We went around the block in this little town and came back. The kid told us that he thought the problem was the fuel pump, so we went into their garage area to look for one.

The man said,

"318 engine, um—I don't think we have anything like that." But as he continued to look on his wooden shelf, he reached way back in and came out with a box. When he opened it, sure enough it contained a fuel pump. He looked it over thoughtfully and said,

"Well, if you use this certain brass fitting…. you know, I believe it will work."

He actually seemed to be surprised that he even had anything like this, and, you know, it did work—perfectly. After it was installed, we took it for a drive around the block and it ran just fine. When I went in to pay him, I said,

"We're praying people and I went past an exit thirty minutes back but when we came to the exit for your town, I just knew that it was the place I needed to get off." I continued, "Where do you suppose would have been the next nearest place that I could have gotten a fuel pump like this?"

He said,

"Well, you came from Spearfish back about 100 miles, and Sioux Falls is another 100 miles that way, so I guess it would have been about a hundred miles, if you even could have found one there."

I said,

"Praise God that we came here and that you took such good care of us."

I paid and thanked him, then we left rejoicing as we continued on our way home, knowing once again that when we obey God and do what He wants us to do, that He's watching over us and will take care of us.

Chapter 11
"One In a Million"

After four days of working in our ten-by-ten booth at the Convention Center in Denver, Colorado, the show came to an end at 1:00 Thursday afternoon. We rushed to disassemble our display booth, packed everything into our motor home, hooked up our car-in-tow, and headed for Ohio some 1200 miles away. With our son-in-law at the wheel of our motor home, I relaxed on one of the back bunks as we traveled down the highway. I looked at the beautiful Rocky Mountains and thought of all that had taken place during the last seven days of the *Christian Booksellers* show, which is a time when Christian bookstore owners/managers shop for new merchandise (my plaques being one of those items).

My mind drifted back to the previous Friday when we arrived in Denver. It was a blistering hot afternoon and all the campgrounds close to town were full, so we called a camp that was about 20 miles from the city. They told us that they had "one electric site" remaining and that they would hold it for us. Praising the Lord for that, we headed for the beautiful Rocky Mountains, but as we started up the first hill our motor home came to a stop. Apparently due to the altitude of the Denver area, we couldn't get the back tank to pump gas through the line since the front tank was already empty. We called for help on our CB and soon a young man with the handle "Cowboy" came and took our son-in-law to get some gas. When they both returned with the gas, "Cowboy" reluctantly took the money I handed him for helping us out. I did manage to ask him,

"If you were to die today, do you know for sure that you would go to Heaven?"

He quickly replied that he didn't, so I handed him the *Four Spiritual Laws* pamphlet and asked him to read it sometime when he was alone. He said that he would, so I shared a few more "quick truths" from God's Word and thanked him again.

It was good to at least have enough gas in the front tank to proceed. Soon we found a gas station and filled up the balance of the two tanks, but we had to leave our car-in-tow at the station because we had forgotten to unhook the battery cables before towing it and the battery had run down. [This was our first experience towing a vehicle behind our motor home, so we didn't realize that we needed to unhook the battery.] We finally arrived at the campground and praised the Lord because this was the last campsite within 50 miles that had electricity and shade, two necessities we dearly needed. However, even the air conditioner didn't help that much in the heat of the day since the temperatures in Denver were near record-setting levels at that time.

Early the next morning, I strolled out of the motor home and viewed the beautiful mountains that God had created. After breakfast, we headed for the Convention Center to set up our booth, which was located on the balcony level. We hired a dockworker to help get our materials to the booth location, and after we unloaded all the materials I walked back with him and started talking to him about God. Again I asked the question,

"If you were to die right now, do you know for sure that you would go to Heaven?"

He said that he didn't even know if there was a Heaven. His name was James, so I handed James a *Four Spiritual Laws* pamphlet, as I often do, and asked him to read it that evening. He said that he would, and then said goodbye. We set up our booth to the point that we were satisfied that it was ready to open on Monday morning, and I silently prayed for James as we headed back toward the beautiful Rocky mountains and our motor home campsite.

After our evening meal, I made my way up the trail to the lodge to inquire about a church in the area that we could attend the next morning, without having to go back into the city. Would you believe that the camp personnel didn't know of even one, though I'm sure there must have been several? As I walked out of the lodge, I asked God to lead me to someone that He wanted me to share with. Farther down the trail, I saw a man sitting by a campfire whittling on a figure of a cowboy. I walked up, introduced myself, and told him that my business was woodworking. After talking shop for a while, the conversation turned to some of my experiences in prison ministry counseling that I had done. Soon his wife, his daughter and her husband, and their teenage son were all listening. When I turned the conversation toward a personal interest in Christ, my audience dwindled down to just the man and his wife. I then asked them the same question I had asked "Cowboy" and James. They both said "No," but added that they did attend church on a regular basis. I inquired,

"Wouldn't you like to know for sure that you're going to Heaven?"

They eagerly replied,

"Yes!"

As we sat there in the cool mountain air by the fire, I shared with them how they could commit their lives to Jesus. I can still picture the evening-silhouetted mountains, the crackling campfire, but most of all I can vividly recall the presence of the Holy Spirit that we felt in those moments as they both committed their lives to Christ.

Sunday we stayed in our motor home and had our fellowship via "TV ministry," after which we crawled into our compact car, which had been fixed by this time, and drove through the mountains. We knew this would likely be our only opportunity to take this beautiful drive because we planned to head back to Ohio as soon as the show was over the following Thursday. We drove into Denver, had dinner, and tried to get tickets for an evening concert that we knew was taking place, but there weren't any tickets left for that performance. Not to be daunted, we found that there was another concert right across the street from the Exhibition Hall where we were. We had our youngest and middle daughters with us, so as we crossed the street I decided to call home and tell our oldest daughter that we had arrived safely, were all set up, and where we were staying. I tried three times to reach her, and on the fourth attempt I felt urged by the Holy Spirit to walk back across the street to the fountain in front of the Exhibition Hall. After she did not answer, I reluctantly walked back across the street and stood at the fountain area in the record-breaking heat, wondering why God had instructed me to do this. I remember staring into the fountain and looking at all the pennies at the bottom, still wondering why I was there. As I sat down on the cement ledge and looked beyond the beautiful frontage of this Exhibition area, I could see the corner stoplights and the people who were casually walking across the street on this hot afternoon.

Suddenly, I thought I saw James, the man who had helped carry our materials to the booth and to whom I had given the *Four Spiritual Laws* tract. While I wasn't positive that it was him, as he was about a block away when I saw him, I felt the Holy Spirit tell me "Go," and so I became convinced that it was James and off I went in hot pursuit, and I do mean "hot." It was almost two-and-a-half blocks before I caught up with him, as he fortunately (for me) had stopped to look in a store window. When I called out to him and he turned around, I exclaimed,

"It is you, James!"

I could see the Four Spiritual Laws tract in his shirt pocket, so I asked if he had read it. He said that he had, but admitted that it had made him even more confused than he was before. [Of course, this is Satan's way of trying to steal the Word, as he is the author of confusion.]

"Where are you going, James?" I asked.

He responded that he was just out walking, so I asked if he would mind if I walked along with him, to which he agreed. As I thought about it later, can you imagine the mathematical odds of me being in just the right place at just the right time to see one particular man cross a specific street in a city of more than a million people? What a glorious feeling it was for me to once again watch God unfold one of His Master Plans!

Because James had come from Ohio, we already had a little something in common to begin with. As we talked, the Holy Spirit seemed to give me specific scriptural answers to James' questions, and, when we stopped occasionally, I could also observe the puzzled faces of people who were overhearing our conversation. As we made our way back to the Exhibition Hall, I explained to him the simple plan of salvation, and, about a block from the Hall, I popped the question:

"James, are you ready to commit your life to Jesus?"

With a hungry look, he said,

"Yes!"

As we stood next to a large downtown building, James became a child of God reborn by the Blood of the Lamb.

James and I walked back to my car where I got a personal Gideon New Testament and an *Introduction to Christian Living* study guide that I gave him. When we returned to the fountain where God had inspired me to start this journey, sitting there was my family. I asked James to tell them what had happened and he said,

"I have been saved by Jesus!"

We praised God together for a few minutes and then headed back to the mountain campsite, praising God all the more for being so absolutely sovereign.

During that week, I had the opportunity to talk to a young lady who was stationed at one of the doors to keep unauthorized people from entering the exhibition area. She seemed very despondent and, I found out later, had backslidden from the Lord. After she had someone relieve her from her assignment one day, we stood in the hallway and she gave her life back to Jesus. The joy of her salvation returned and her sadness turned to radiance. She was still smiling several days later when we said our goodbye to Denver.

As I looked back at Denver and the beautiful Rocky Mountains from our motor home window, I knew that God had permitted me to leave a little bit of myself there in Denver, and a lot of Jesus. God is such a good God, and we praise Him for letting us share Jesus with those who do not yet know him, as well as those who once did.

Chapter 12
"God Heals Even Via TV"

A friend of ours, who had been a nurse for a number of years, started having digestive problems. As it worsened, she found that she could eat only soft foods, such as those that a small baby would eat. It seemed that the doctors couldn't do anything more for her. I received a call from her one evening and she was praising the Lord. She proceeded to tell me that the morning before, after her husband had left for work, she decided that she couldn't go on this way any longer. (I am not sure exactly what she meant by that statement.) She had sat down and turned on the television and started flipping through the channels. The *700 Club* program was on and Pat Robertson and Ben Kinchlow were praying for peoples' needs. All of a sudden, Pat said,

"There is a woman out there that has a throat and heart problem. No, it's an esophagus problem, and God has just healed you."

She got up from her chair, went to the kitchen and made herself a large breakfast, one that she normally could not eat. Because she had been instantly and totally healed, she was able to eat it <u>and</u> keep it down. A number of years ago they moved to another state.

Bud checking Gertrude's accuracy. Bud made these archery bows.

Chapter 13
"Go To Lugbill's"

A long time ago I gave up trying to figure out why God works in unusual and different ways. I have come to the conclusion that the only thing He desires from us is to simply be obedient. As we read the Bible, we find that God did things very differently on many occasions and as you read this story you will see that He hasn't stopped doing things in His perfect, though unusual at times, way.

I was working at my drawing board doing artwork for some of our award trophies when I thought I heard a voice say,

"Go to *Lugbill Town*."

As our little town was expanding, they had moved the corporation limits farther to the South to include what we called *Lugbill Town* where there were a few homes and businesses. [Some of us "old timers" still call it *Lugbill Town*, although it has since been incorporated into the municipality of Archbold.] While I don't often do this, I ignored the voice because I thought it was "just me." Then the second time the voice repeated,

"Go to *Lugbill Town*."

I again brushed it off thinking,

"I'm just imagining all this."

The third time it was so loud in my head that I jumped up and actually said,

"Yes Sir!"

It was around 5:00 P.M. and time to go home anyhow, so I went out to my car and drove to *Lugbill Town*. Though *Lugbill Town* wasn't exactly on my way home, I drove the three miles out there. When I stopped at the traffic light, I said,

"Lord, where should I go?"

As there was no response, I turned around and started back home, but when I stopped at the next traffic light, the voice said,

"Go to Wes's place."

My good friend Wes, with whom I had gone through school and who had been in our wedding, had a separate building off to the side of his house where he fixed wrecked cars. I quickly replied,

"Lord, I was just at Wes's house this morning."

So I started for home when the voice said,

"I said, Go to Wes's!"

And for the second time, I said,

"Yes Sir!!"

When I walked into Wes's garage, he was talking to a young Christian man that I knew. I still wondered,

"Why am I here?"

I just leaned back on the bench, waiting for exactly what I didn't know. Suddenly the door opened and in came a man in his late thirties. I wasn't sure who he was until we started talking. The conversation soon turned to spiritual things and, at that, Wes walked over to us. As it turned out, before Wes started his own business he had worked with this man for years.

In a matter of minutes, the man asked Jesus into his life and became a child of God. As we continued talking, I related the story as to why I had come here at this particular time and how the Lord had so strongly insisted that I do so. What he said next was nothing short of amazing, at least to me. He said that he was within half a mile of his home, about three miles past Wes's place, when he heard a voice telling him that he should turn around and go back to Wes's place.

"That is why I am here," he said.

Then it all finally made sense. I look back to that day and wonder,

"What if *I* hadn't been obedient to the Spirit's voice?"

"What if _he_ hadn't responded to the Holy Spirit's voice and turned around?"

"Why did I have to go to _Lugbill Town_ and then start back toward home before the Spirit's voice returned?"

I have come to the conclusion that God wanted to see if I was willing to <u>continue</u> obeying Him, even when it was not making sense to me. I wonder how many times I have failed to obey God's leading and whether He had to send someone else in my place? I know that God's way always makes sense, regardless of what I think.

This story ends in a rather unusual way because, about two years after his conversion, this same man lost his life in a freak accident. I thank God that both of us obeyed that voice when we were given instructions. When we hear the Spirit's voice, I am sure that we are the only ones that hear that voice—so listen carefully, and obey when He speaks!

Chapter 14
"The Unlisted Number"

During a prison crusade with the Bill Glass group in a South Carolina State prison, I had an unusual answer to prayer. I had already had a number of unusual events that happened that weekend, but this one ended differently yet. During the weekend I had become friends with an inmate named Tommy who had been born again before the crusade came to that prison. Because he loved to minister to other inmates, the officials kept moving him from dorm to dorm. He accompanied me during that weekend and took me to different people with whom he wanted me to talk. Then on the last day of the crusade he told me about a problem he had. He said that he had been married and had a couple of children. Since he was about 30 years old, I knew that the children had to be fairly young. He told me that his wife had divorced him and remarried, but that he wanted to call her and inquire about their children. The problem was that she had an unlisted phone number, which he didn't know, and that when he wrote to her she would simply return his letters. This made Tommy very frustrated as he felt that he had no hope of talking to her or his children. After telling me his story I said,

"Tommy, let's just ask God to get you that unlisted number."

I could tell by his expression that he had never reached out that far in faith for such a prayer request. I just laid my hand on Tommy and simply asked God to get that unlisted number for him. (Years later in Hawaii God got us an unlisted number as told about in our Hawaii story.)

About two weeks after returning home from the crusade, I received a call from Tommy at our place of business. At his prison they had pay phones that inmates could use to make outgoing calls with tokens they purchased with money from their account held by the prison. Tommy was on the phone laughing and crying at the same time, so much so that it was difficult to understand what he was trying to tell me. I said,

"Tommy calm down! I can't understand you!"

When he finally calmed down, he told me the following story.

Bud," he said, "I just hung up from talking to my former wife and she has filled me in on everything about our children!" He continued, "I first called the operator to get her number and, as I expected, the operator said, 'I'm sorry sir, but that number is unlisted,' at which I replied, "Yes ma'am, I know it is." But to my surprise she said, 'Here it is,' and gave me the number." He said, "I was so taken off guard that I just stood by the phone in disbelief. I then decided that I would dial the operator again to see what would happen. I got a different operator this time who repeated word for word what the first operator had said about the number being unlisted, but then gave me the same number. I knew then that it had to be an answer to our prayer, so I dialed that number and my former wife answered. She said, 'Tommy, how did you get this number?' I told her that she wouldn't believe it. I just asked her about our children and she answered all of my questions. I hung up, praised the Lord, and knew that I had to call you."

I often have wondered what those two operators thought when they realized what they had done, or maybe God erased it from their minds so they wouldn't have to feel guilty about it. Either way, we know that God was in control. That was the last contact I had with Tommy, but I am sure that answer to prayer boosted his faith, as it did mine, and has kept him on the right road. God continues to amaze me with His love and compassion. He knew how much Tommy loved his children and satisfied his questions of concern for them by allowing Tommy to talk to his wife—even though the number was unlisted. God is interested in every aspect of our lives. As the little chorus goes, "God is so good," and I have to agree.

In this age of computers, Tommy would have been talking to a computer that couldn't give the number unless God worked an even greater miracle, which He certainly can.

Chapter 15
"Gertrude's Death Row Experiences"

It was time for another Bill Glass prison crusade and so, with twelve counselors aboard our motor home; we left for the state of Texas. The first few crusades, I did most of the driving with Gertrude in the "co-pilot's" seat, but then we devised a plan where we changed drivers and co-pilots every two hours so there was always a fresh driver and partner up front. Twenty-six hours after our departure from Archbold, we arrived at our motel in Texas where crusade counselors from all over the United States headquarter at the same motel. First-time counselors must attend a training session on Thursday night and, since we always had a "freshman" counselor or two, we arrived early on Thursday. Friday mornings were for orientation, devotions, prayer, and assignments as to which prison we would be sent. After a quick lunch, we men were bussed to our assigned prisons and the ladies were bussed to the women's prison.

There are always enough Christian celebrities and athletes to alternate their programs to the prisons. After they give their testimonies, they say,

"There are people here who have come at their own expense to talk with you if you are interested."

They add,

"Counselors, stand up and hold your packets high so they can see who and where you are."

There are always some prisoners in special lock-down units that are not allowed to attend these programs. In those cases, veteran counselors are selected to visit them in their cells. Since the rest of this is Gertrude's story, I will have her tell it.

At the time, this particular woman's prison did not have a separate death row unit. It was instead located on the lower level in an isolated area at the end of a long row of cells where the difficult inmates were kept who, for various reasons, were not allowed with the other inmates. We were warned that some of these prisoners in lock-down were very dangerous and that we should not get near their cells or they might grab us. On Friday I had dealt with many girls. Some had previously become Christians in jail and were hungry for other Christians just to talk to. One such girl asked if she could please talk to me again the next day. I told her that I had been assigned to death row and the lock-down section, and therefore would not be able to talk to her. She then excitedly asked that when I visited Susan, the only woman on death row, I should tell her that the other Christians loved her and were praying for her. [Susan had become a Christian in prison.] As I headed down the long row of cells, girls were begging me to stop and talk to them, but I told them that I needed to start at the other end and would eventually work my way back. Then I encountered something I never had before, or since—a woman screaming and cursing at me from one of the cells. The Holy Spirit confirmed to my spirit that this was not just foul language, but was from the very pit of hell itself. I knew that this woman needed deliverance before she could accept Christ, though Bill Glass counselors are instructed not to get into deliverance. I would have been tempted to stay home had I known what I was about to encounter.

A few days before we left on the crusade, I read a book on "Demons and Deliverance" that a friend had loaned me. Since our church never had any teaching on this, as I was reading the book I asked to meet with our pastor. Just before I left his office, I remember saying,

"I surely hope that the Lord never asks me to come up against a demon."

He very gently said,

"Sister, if you do, just do whatever the Lord tells you."

The book said that we are to rebuke the foul spirits with authority. As this inmate continued screaming and cursing me, I very quietly, but firmly and with authority, commanded the foul spirit to be still in the NAME OF JESUS, and continued past a few empty cells to visit Susan. I introduced myself to Susan and gave her the message from the other Christian inmates. After praying with her and bidding her goodbye, she called to the one who had cursed at me to please talk with me. The screaming began again, but Susan persisted saying,

"Tell her about your dream. You asked me for help and I told you that I could not help you, but I would pray for God to send someone who could. I believe this lady is that person—if you will let her."

I will call this inmate Beulah, though that is not her real name. As I reached Beulah's cell, she was very rude and belligerent. After several attempts to talk to her, and since there were other girls waiting to talk with me, I pointed my finger at her and said,

"DO YOU WANT HELP? DO YOU WANT TO CHANGE?"

Immediately she got quiet and said,

"I had a dream. I saw myself sitting in a rowboat in a swamp where very slimy creatures surrounded me and were trying to grab me. They said, 'We are demons and you are one also.' I kept screaming for help when an angel reached down from heaven and said, "DO YOU WANT HELP? DO YOU WANT TO CHANGE?"

I marveled that those were the exact words I had spoken to her. When she told me that, Holy Spirit bumps came on my arms, and I knew why God had put it in my heart to study that book about demons and deliverance.

I then said to her,

"God did not send an angel, but He did send this vessel of clay all the way from Ohio to tell you about Jesus, that He loves you and wants to deliver and save you."

We never ask inmates about their crimes, but we listen if they tell us. If they do, we then tell them that God is ready to forgive them if they will only repent and accept Jesus. She proceeded to tell me that she was thirty years old and that the only thing she had ever accomplished was graduating from high school. She and her boyfriend were into drugs and did horrible things, the likes of which I cannot write here. I explained to her the plan of salvation but, when she tried to pray, she could not. I felt led to ask her if there was someone that she had not forgiven. She said,

"Yes, I will never forgive my mother because the last time she visited me she said, 'I hope that you die in here.'"

I told her that if she did not forgive her mother, she was breaking the bridge for her own forgiveness. After I rebuked the spirit of unforgiveness, she still could not accept Christ or forgive her Mother. Again I asked her to follow me in a prayer. I said,

"God, you know that I cannot forgive my Mother, but with your help I will."

After repeated attempts, she triumphantly said,

"With your help, I will forgive my Mother. I will forgive my mother!"

She was then able to repent and accept Christ. As she wept, I put my arms through the bars and hugged her. I left her literature and shared more of God's word with her, and also promised to write her, which I did. She wrote to me and told me that she was now permitted to be with the other inmates and was working in the rose garden (my favorite flower—I have some in my flower garden). She was also working on her weight and appearance. The devil had tried to destroy her so I had to break the rules and attempt to deliver her on behalf of Christ. I would not advise anyone to do this unless they have the Word of God deeply imbedded in them, and are armed with the power of the Holy Spirit, as you are walking right into Satan's territory. Remember that Jesus told us that Satan comes to STEAL, KILL AND DESTROY, but HE, JESUS, came to give us life and to give it to us more abundantly (John 10:10).

After visiting and sharing with the other girls in that lock-down section, I immediately went to my supervisor and told him what had happened. He told me not to worry about it and rejoiced with me. The Bill Glass crusades are a wonderful and much needed ministry outreach. I believe it would do everyone good to go on at least one; however, we do not go to them anymore since we provide Sunday morning services in our large five-county jail and are involved there.

Chapter 16
"No Altar Call"

Before we started wintering in the South, from time to time I would receive requests to fill in for pastors for various reasons. A pastor friend of mine, who decided to go back to college for some additional training, needed someone to preach at his small country church for a Sunday or two, so one of the elders from the church called me and asked if I would be willing to do the preaching, to which I readily agreed. It wasn't like I was a complete stranger to the church anyhow because my family had sung there on several occasions in the past. Several years later when their pastor resigned, I was asked to once again fill in for several Sundays until a new pastor could be found, which "fill in" request turned into a six-month interim position for me, through no fault of anyone.

One Sunday morning, just before I got up to minister, the same elder who had called me stood up and said to the congregation,

"It's good to have our former pastor here visiting with us this morning."

The former pastor stood up, spoke a few words of greeting, and then sat back down. As I approached the pulpit, I invited the former pastor to give one of his sermons, but he declined and so I proceeded with mine. Generally, it is my custom to give an altar call after preaching, but that morning, for some reason, I didn't particularly feel led to do that, so I didn't. Instead, I took my place at the back of the church where I asked the former pastor to join me in greeting the people as they left the sanctuary. Among those whom we greeted were two ladies who stopped to tell me that they worked in a turnpike restaurant together and passed out tracts whenever they could. After the crowd had passed by, the Holy Spirit spoke to me and said that one of those two ladies who worked at the turnpike restaurant was not saved. I turned to the former pastor and asked,

"What are the names of those two ladies who work at the restaurant?"

He named the one as a member of the church, but said that the other lady had visited there only a couple of times and he didn't know her name.

I rushed out the door to search for this lady and quickly found her out near the front of the church. I saw that she had just gotten into her car, and as I approached her she rolled down the window. I don't remember the first thing I said, but I do know I asked her,

"Do you know Jesus as your Savior?"

At this point she burst into tears and said,

"No, I don't."

"Do you want to know Him?" I said.

"Yes, yes!" she cried out.

I took her back into the church and invited the former pastor to join us in the pastor's study where she came to know Jesus as her Savior.

I have learned that when the Holy Spirit speaks, I had better obey. John 13:16 says, "The Holy Spirit will guide you into all truth." The point to this story is that I was later told by a friend in that church that she was praying that a certain lady in the congregation that morning would get saved during my usual altar call. She said that she was shocked when I closed the service without even giving an invitation. As you probably have guessed, the lady that I ran out to talk to in the parking lot who gave her life to Christ in the pastor's study was the one that my friend had been praying would be saved that morning. The Holy Spirit merely had another way to bring that dear lady to Christ.

Chapter 17
"Glory Row!"

Though I earlier related a story about one of my Bill Glass crusade experiences, let me tell you how it all started. In 1975, I decided that I was going to pray about getting involved in the Bill Glass prison crusade ministry. I had heard all kinds of things about prisons, and even saw in the newspapers how prisoners would often riot, so after about six weeks of praying I was still a little nervous about the decision. As Gertrude and I still had **THE GOSPEL HITS** motor home that we used when our family traveled and did some singing, I decided to take about ten fellows with me and go down to the Marion, Ohio prison facility for a Bill Glass weekend prison crusade. For the reader's sake, I want to make the point that as we left the corporation limits of Archbold (why it was at that particular point in the road, I don't know) absolutely all fear about prisons left me and I have <u>never</u> had any fear of ministering in a prison since. I heard some Christian counselors say that 'you've got to have some measure of fear when you go into a prison,' but all fear left me when I stepped out in faith. As II Timothy 1:7 tells us, "God has not given us the spirit of fear, but (the spirit) of love and of a sound mind." I have been locked in Death Row facilities as a counselor, and there are many stories that go with that, but I have never had any fear whatsoever. Following is a rather special story of one of my Bill Glass prison crusade experiences.

We were in the center of the Oklahoma State Prison, which had a large rodeo arena where the inmates and invited guests held rodeos and other types of programs. As the first program was about to begin, and as I (Bud) often do, I "picked out" an inmate to sit next to. However, as I sat down, I felt the urging of the Holy Spirit to move further down into the bleacher area. So I got up and moved, wondering how far down I should sit, when I heard the Holy spirit say,

"All the way to the front!"

I was mumbling to myself about being so far down, but, knowing that there must be a good reason, I moved all the way down to the front and sat by an inmate. Again I heard that voice say,

"This man has a bitter spirit and you must pray for him."

I heard the words quite clearly, but remember wondering to myself just how I was going to do that. I was sort of relieved, for the moment at least, because the program was just beginning.

A few hours earlier, as the ten of us were traveling across the hot prairie of Oklahoma in our motor home, little did I know that this was going to be the most challenging crusade I had ever attended. As the miles seemed to drag on in the nearly unbearable heat, our air conditioner did little to alleviate the humidity and the uncomfortableness inside our 'bus.' When we finally saw the *Holiday Inn* come into view, everyone rejoiced! We pulled in, the fellows grabbed their suitcases and headed for the sign-in desk, and in a matter of minutes they were all in the pool. After I parked, as Gertrude wanted me out of the way so she could clean up the motor home from ten guys being inside, it didn't take me long to don my swimsuit and join the rest of the guys in the pool. When I got there, they were talking to a big six-foot-eight-inch Texan in the middle of the pool. I just sat on the edge with my feet dangling in the cool water listening to their conversation about spiritual matters. All of a sudden a hush seemed to come over the pool with no one saying anything. I thought to myself,

"Is this witnessing going to stop here?"

I was about 30 feet from the big Texan so I called out,

"What's your name?"

"Larry," he replied.

So I asked,

"Larry, if you were to die right now, do you know for sure that you would go to Heaven?"

He quickly replied with a positive answer, but with what I thought was just some memorized "church doctrine" statement. So I came back with a second question,

"Larry, if you were to stand in front of God right now and He were to say, 'Why should I let you into My Heaven?' what would you tell him?"

As he seemed to answer with just more church doctrine, I jumped into the pool, waded over to him, and said,

"Larry, I have some good news for you."

The fellows surrounded Larry and me and prayed silently as I proceeded to share with Larry the plan of salvation. When I finished that, I asked him if he wanted to commit his life to Jesus and he replied,

"Yes, I do."

Right there in the middle of the pool, this big Texan, who was a former college basketball star, became born again. I asked,

"Larry, if you were to die right now, where would you wake up?"

Without hesitation he said,

"In Heaven!"

Immediately I came back with

"How do you know?"

He surprised us all by shouting,

"Praise the Lord, I've been born again!"

He went on to explain that he was an engineer and that he and his wife had spent some time in New York where she had attended a Bible study and had been born again. He went to the Bible study with her one night, but thought they were taking their "religion" too serious and never went back. But on this day he was like a ripe apple ready to fall from the tree, and we just happened to be there to catch him. He jumped out of the pool and rushed to his room to call his wife in Houston to give her the good news.

The next afternoon @ 1:00 PM we were off to the prison for the first program of the weekend. After going through tight security, we found ourselves in the middle of the prison and the largest rodeo arena I have ever seen. As I mentioned at the outset, I was seated beside an inmate whom, I had been told by the Lord, was very bitter. We are required to be attentive and respectful of the program itself, so I only had time to say "Hello." The Holy Spirit was reminding me that this inmate had a bitter spirit and that I was to pray for him. Indeed he did have a bitter spirit, for at that moment he and his two friends poured out a few bitter exclamations. I watched attentively as the athletes performed and gave their testimonies. While this particular program was not a rodeo, it was held in that spacious arena because the facility accommodated so many spectators (prisoners and counselors). The men and women performing/participating in the arena included some of the best record-holding Christian athletes in the world from football, basketball, weight lifting, track and field, etc. During the program I was asking the Lord to "glue that man to his seat" when the program was over so that I could talk with him, but I kept wondering exactly what I was going to say. The program ended and one of the guest athletes jumped over the fence right there within six feet of us. I thought that surely the inmate sitting next to me would jump up for an autograph and that my chance to talk to him would be gone. However, at that point the inmate's two friends said something to him and then crowded around the guest, leaving the inmate, more or less, "glued to his seat."

As I turned to him and asked,

"Would you like to talk?"

To my amazement, he said

"Sure." [Why was I amazed?]

After we introduced ourselves (his name was Leon), the conversation turned to him. He said,

"I am a very bitter person."

I quickly replied,

"Yes, I know, because God revealed that to me when I sat down beside you earlier. He also said that I am to pray for you."

Out of the blue he said to me,

"Do you think this bitter spirit is kind of like a demon."

"Yes," I replied, "like a demon."

When I asked if I could pray for him, he consented. I put my arm around his shoulder and rebuked the bitter spirit in the name of Jesus. When the prayer was finished he looked at me with relief on his face as he said,

"I feel so different—like something is gone on the inside."

I went on to explain that since he had been delivered of the bitter spirit, he needed to replace it with Jesus. After quoting some scripture and telling him the story of the "clean house" of Matthew 12:43, I explained to him the plan of salvation, at which he opened the door of his heart and asked Christ to come in. He then invited me back to his cell to see some photos of his family. As I sat on a bunk looking at his family album, in walked a hulk of a man. He was so large that he had to bend over to get through the door and I jumped up quickly when Leon told me that I was sitting on this man's bunk. Leon introduced me, and, after he sat down on his bunk, I asked him if anyone had talked to him about Jesus.

"They wouldn't want to do that," he replied.

When I asked him why, he opened his shirt collar and showed me a chain with a cross that was hung upside down. I told him that while the cross meant something to me, I didn't know why it was hung upside down.

"It's because I'm a Satan worshipper," he said, attempting to overpower me with his words. As I stated previously, I had absolutely no fear whatsoever of going into prisons as the Lord had delivered me from that harmful emotion.

I had never met a professing Satan worshipper before.
I said, "You're a what?"
He repeated,
"A Satan worshipper."
I asked,
"What do you mean, a Satan worshipper?"
He answered,
"You know what I mean—Satan, the devil."
I took out my pocket Bible and asked,
"You mean the Satan from this book?"
He looked straight at me and said,
"Yea, that's the one."
To this I replied,
"Man, do you ever have me confused. I can't understand how you believe that part of this book and don't believe the rest."

He stared at me with a puzzled look on his face, so I knew that the Holy Spirit was convicting him. I carried the conversation as far as the Holy Spirit took me, but then I stopped abruptly. I had seen the cell door closing, but didn't know that it wouldn't open again for another hour and a half. Since we were all three 'captive' for the next ninety minutes,

I sat there and listened to the big man and Leon tell me all about their families. Having said all that I felt I could say, and with no apparent fruit of my efforts, I left Leon and his cellmate and headed for the chow line when the doors finally opened.

There I met and ate with a young man named Rick who told me that he was 28 years old and already had been married five times.

"Five?" I said questioning, "and you're only 28? Wow, you must have started young."

As we sat in the yard, he started to tell me about his first wife. After a few minutes, I interrupted him,

"Rick, this sounds like a soap opera that could take the whole weekend and I'm here to talk about Jesus. Would you like to hear about him?"

He responded,

"Yes," and about 20 minutes later Rick received Christ.

I found out that he had been singing in the prison choir and had been seeking Christ, which reminded me of the scripture in Jeremiah 29:13 that says, "You shall seek me, and you shall find me, when you search for me with all your heart."

To insert this, six weeks after I returned home I received a letter from Rick. As I read it, tears ran down my cheeks. It read as follows:

"God has healed my mother's eyes! The doctor was going to do surgery but the day before she was to go into the hospital she came to see me. I laid hands on her and asked God to heal her. I told the devil to let her go in the name of Jesus our Lord and Savior. The next day she went into the hospital. The eye doctor came and got her and when the surgeon looked at her eyes, he told the eye doctor that he could not see anything wrong with her eyes. The eye doctor looked and he could not see anything either. My mother told them that God had healed her eyes. They checked her vision and she had 20/20. I give God the praise."

No one had told Rick that it might not work, so he asked God in childlike faith to heal his mother because he had read John 14:12-14 and believed it.

After I left Rick, I was walking across the yard when I came upon a group of inmates, and felt the Lord directing me to talk to the one in the center. I introduced myself and he told me that his name was Bill. When I talked to him about Jesus, he said that he was not ready for anything like that yet. I asked if I could pray for him, to which he consented. I simply put my arm around his shoulder and asked for victory in his life. When I had finished, I told him that I would be hearing from him soon telling me how Jesus had come into his life. I did not see him anymore during the crusade, but I later received this letter:

"Bud—when you told me that Jesus would come into my life, I thought you were crazy. That day you said that sometime real soon Jesus would save me and you were right. Praise the Lord, Jesus has come into my life and what a wonderful feeling."

I have heard from Bill several times since and he was always praising the Lord.

Saturday morning all of us counselors gathered in the center of the rotunda at the prison where several doors led to different cellblocks, with the various cellblocks identified by a name over each door. One door had the name "Death Row" over it, and I knew that the Lord wanted me to go in there. When our group leader asked for five volunteers for Death Row, I happened to be standing up in front of the group, facing them but behind our group leader, Bob Cole, who was also facing the group. As I raised my hand behind him, I thought, "Lord, I'm sure that you want me to go in there." Bob hurriedly said, "I'll take you, you, you and you" as he pointed his finger in rapid succession to four men directly in front of him, and then whirled around and said, "And Bud, you go." Wow, the Lord did it again! [By the way, Bob Cole was a former conman and gambler, known as Bull Cole, and part of the movie *The Sting* is from his own life.] As the five of us were ushered into Death Row, a strange feeling came over me for a moment as the doors closed behind us. We were allowed to walk right up to the individual cell doors, which would then be opened for a counselor to go in and sit down with the inmate, and for the next five hours we were all locked in Death Row. As we walked to the far end of the long walkway, one of the inmates urged me to stop and talk with him, but I just assured him that I would be back since we had been asked to start at the far end of the walkway and then work our way back to where we came in. The cells were about six feet wide by ten feet long and consisted of a bunk, sink, commode, and a hanging 60-watt light bulb. Because all their meals were brought to them, these inmates in Death Row rarely got out of their cells. The first cell I walked up to revealed an inmate reading a paperback. I told him who we were and why we were there, all of which did not seem to impress him. As I was talking to him, the Holy Spirit revealed to me his past church affiliation and the name of it. To his amazement (and mine) it was correct, and that seemed to get his attention. He not only listened to what I had to say, but also eventually accepted Christ into his life that day.

I moved to the next cell, and once again the Holy Spirit revealed this inmate's church background, which was, again, correct. In the Bill Glass prison crusades, we use the *Four Spiritual Laws* guide exclusively and then leave it with the prisoner. As I started down the list of those four spiritual laws with this prisoner, I explained, in turn, how that

(i) God loved him and had a plan for his life,

(ii) That all persons have sinned and are in need of forgiveness, and

(iii) That God's only provision for salvation and eternal life is through Jesus Christ.

The point of my saying it in this way is that I was truly surprised at what came out of my mouth next. I heard myself saying,

"Now when Moses was in Egypt, all the firstborn were to be slain unless there was blood over the door."

At that moment a spiritual conversation took place between me and the Lord.

"What's going on?" I asked the Lord. "I'm looking at one thing on this tract and my mouth is saying something else—help me to understand!"

Yet, instead of going to the fourth spiritual law as outlined in the tract, I found myself going through the complete Passover story as given in the book of Exodus. When I finished telling the story, Bobby, who was the inmate, cried out

"That's it! I need the blood over my cell door just like those people! I've got it! I've got it! I know what you're telling me!"

While he was excitedly telling me that, I'm thinking,

"Tell me, then we will both know!"

He exclaimed, "You're telling me that the blood of Jesus can save me—praise the Lord!"

I finally understood his need for protection; so I went on to explain the whole plan of salvation. After Bobby accepted the Lord, he laughed and cried simultaneously. In his letters he still talked about Moses, but, better still, he talks about Jesus. [Three months after Bobby accepted the Lord, he was taken off Death Row and became an assistant to the prison chaplain, another miracle in itself.]

As I proceeded back down the walkway of cells, I led a nineteen-year-old man to Jesus next. As I continued my way back, I came to the man who had called out to me on my way in. Rick introduced himself and told me that he had been saved two weeks earlier. A lady from California had been sending him letters and literature for months telling him all about Jesus and how he could be saved. He said that after many months he finally got down on his knees and gave himself to Jesus. I rejoiced with him over this and we talked and prayed. The Holy Spirit seemed to insist that I pray for him to receive the infilling of the Holy Spirit; however, I was not very comfortable telling that to a new Christian on Death Row. As I mentally argued,

"Lord, he won't have the slightest notion what I'm talking about,"

Rick interrupted me and said,

"The lady who has been writing to me told me that what I need now is 'The Baptism of the Holy Spirit'."

I responded,

"That is what I was going to tell you, Rick. The Lord asked me to pray for you to receive this gift."

At this he dropped to his knees, as I did also, and I laid my hands upon him to receive the infilling of the Holy Spirit. The praise goes to God for the mighty power of His Holy Spirit and how much He loves these inmates when their hearts are sincere and hungry for Him.

From that day on, the inmates changed the name of "Death Row" to "Glory Row," and all the letters I received from that place had Death Row crossed out (~~Death Row~~) and "Glory Row" written in. A revival broke out in Glory Row after we left and many more inmates were saved. A Bible study also began, which Rick himself led. Even though they cannot see each other, being strictly confined to their cells, God has blessed their Bible study. Rick wrote me asking for an old Bible with a concordance in it so that he could pass it around to the other Glory Row inmates. I was able to do even better than that. Our church responded and we sent a large box of old Bibles with concordances, along with a few new ones.

Since we were there, the officials had begun to allow the prisoners to attend chapel a few times.

The Lord Jesus Christ, through many different groups, is invading prisons all across America because He is the only true way that lives can be changed. We do not go into prisons to rehabilitate those inmates; we go to regenerate them through Jesus Christ with the new life that is in <u>Him</u>. Colossians 3:9b-10 says, "Seeing that you have put off the old man with his deeds … put on the new man which is renewed in knowledge after the image of him that created him." Because all Bill Glass crusades conclude after each Sunday morning service, the next day the announcement was made that we counselors had five minutes to exit before the gates would be locked. I was talking to another inmate when my partner said,

"Bud, we have only a few minutes to get out of here."

As I worked my way down the row of bleachers, I spied the big Satan worshipper two rows up. Immediately I went up, grabbed his hand, and said,

"It's good to see you again, but I have to go now."

He mumbled something I didn't quite understand as tears started to roll down his cheeks. I only pray that this Satan worshipper became a God worshipper.

Occasionally I would write a general letter to "Glory Row" for all the inmates to pass around and read. About three and a half years after the Glory Row experiences, I received a call from Bobby praising the Lord. He told me that there were eight Bible studies going on, with even more to begin. We had decided to visit our youngest daughter and her husband in Tulsa, so when Bobby called the next time we made arrangements to get visitation rights so that Gertrude and I could travel the additional 142 miles from Tulsa to visit him. When we were taken to the visiting room, Bobby's mother, a Christian, was there, and what a glorious time we had for three hours listening to Bobby's excitement and knowledge of the Bible. After about an hour, I turned to Bobby's mother and asked her if she had ever been filled with the Holy Spirit. When she said no, I asked her if she would like to. Without hesitation she said,

"Yes!"

Without delay she instantly received God's gift.

Chapter 18
"The Lump is Gone!"

A number of years ago we hosted some Bible Studies in our basement, led primarily by a Spanish-American pastor friend of ours. After each study session, it was our custom to pray for any needs of those who had come. On one occasion, someone brought a lady to be prayed for who had a lump about the size of a golf ball protruding out of her neck. As it happened, a young man who had heard about this Bible Study came on that same night to see what it was all about. During the prayer for this lady, my pastor friend laid his hand on the lump, which we suspected was a goiter, and said,

"Go, in the name of Jesus!"

When he removed his hand, the lump was gone!

The young man cried out,

"My God, it's gone!"

Needless to say, it was life changing for him just as it was for the rest of us.

The following week the young man came back and brought his wife along. As they walked into the basement room where the Bible Studies were held, my wife, Gertrude did a very unusual thing—for her, at least. She walked over to him, placed her hand on his head, and said,

"I am to pray for you—be healed in the name of Jesus."

It was approximately five years later that he and his wife happened to be at the same church that we were and, as we walked out together after the service, he said,

"I have never told you this, but do you remember the night you prayed for me at the Bible Study? I was healed and the problem has never come back.

His wife verified that her husband had that problem from childhood and that he hasn't been bothered with that condition since that night. Gertrude replied,

"I didn't know what I was praying for, only that I was to pray."

There isn't anything too big or too small to ask God for, when we ask it in the Name of Jesus. God is so good!

Chapter 19
"He Gave it all to Jesus!"

A few years ago, on a cold, crisp evening, I left my office about 5:30 to get some supplies at our local hardware store before it closed for the day. I arrived just as the clerks were closing down for the day, but I was permitted to get the supplies that I needed. After Tom, the manager and part owner, checked me out, he indicated that he had something he wanted to talk to me about.

In our small rural community, we know most of the family backgrounds of the people who were raised there. I knew Tom's family background and that he was the store's manager, but I did not know him personally. As the clerks had left for the day and locked the doors behind them, Tom started asking me questions about the Bill Glass prison ministry. He knew that I was involved in it and just wanted to know more about it. A few days earlier a mutual friend had given a presentation to a small group where he had shown some prison slides and Tom had been present. The Lord had kept this on Tom's mind for several days, so he decided to ask me about it. Little did I realize the plan that God started working out that afternoon.

The phone rang after we had been talking a few minutes, and it was Tom's wife inquiring when he would be home, so he hurriedly got to the point.

"I would really like to go on a prison crusade," he said very sincerely, "but I wouldn't know how to talk to the inmates."

I tried to assure him that the Lord can use any willing heart, if they will but ask Him for help. He began to unload a burden that was weighing on him.

"Bud," he said, "I have been saved since I was a young man, and have always loved the Lord."

He went on to tell me how he had always been faithful in going to church and living a good, clean moral life. With tears in his eyes he then said,

"I am a Sunday School teacher and thirty-two years old, but I've never led anyone to Jesus."

Since he had just confessed to a brother what was on his heart, the Lord's plan was now put into action.

Tom's case is so typical. Many think that living the good life and serving in the church are the only things that are required, but Jesus said, "The fields are white for harvest." We must begin to harvest souls before Satan brings his spiritual hailstorm and flattens the ripe grain of their hearts. Someone once said that we shouldn't buttonhole people by talking to them too aggressively about Christ, but I say that it is better to buttonhole them into Heaven than to ignore them and see them go to Hell.

"Tom," I urged, "why don't you come with us to the jail ministry on Saturday morning with the Gideon's?"

Tom was a Gideon, but was never involved in our local jail ministry. He agreed to go to our prayer breakfast the following Saturday. At the Prayer Breakfast on Saturday morning, Tom said to me,

"The devil sure tried to stop me this morning. One of my clerks was sick, but God took care of it." (Another clerk came in to work in Tom's place.)

I knew that I had some work to do at the office after the prayer breakfast on Saturday, so I told him that I would meet him and the others at the jail at 9:30.

Tom was there at the jail and I told him to tag along and observe how the Holy Spirit prepares the hearts of the men that we talk to. We went to the second floor and there back in a dimly lighted corner stood a young man in a small cell. We talked to him for a few minutes and shared the love of Christ with him; however, he politely refused to accept the Lord, saying that he was not yet ready to do that. My heart always aches when I hear this. How much more must the Lord's heart ache with a love that human hearts cannot even comprehend. As we walked over to another cell, I told Tom that I had been witnessing to this man, Gary, for over three months but that he was still rejecting Christ.

Though Gary had gone to Sunday School as a boy, and therefore knew some of the basic Bible stories, he had come from a broken home and still harbored some very bad memories. He was also a Vietnam veteran with a drug and alcohol abuse problem. I looked back into the cell and called out,

"Good morning, Gary!" and, as I did, Gary came over to the door.

He looked very pale and was holding on to the wall for support.

"What's wrong, Gary?" I asked. "You don't look like you're doing very well today."

After I introduced Tom, Gary told us that they had taken him to the doctor but that they couldn't find out what was wrong.

"Gary," I said, "let's ask God to heal you in the name of Jesus."

It was new to Tom for me to just boldly claim John 14:14 where Jesus said, "Ask anything in My Name and I will do it." As I said this, Gary laid his hand on the food platform of the cell door and I laid my hand on his. I knew that Tom wanted to get in on this because he then laid his hand on mine. Tom was one step down from the cell at the top of the stairs and was kneeling on one knee as I started to pray for Gary's healing. Then I asked the Holy Spirit to come upon Gary and reveal the truth of Jesus Christ to him. As I was claiming these promises of God, I became aware that Gary was sobbing softly. It was then that the "Holy Spirit bumps" began to come all over my body, and they really got big when I realized that Tom was sniffling a bit, too. I knew that something beautiful was about to happen to both Tom and Gary.

The moment I said "Amen," Tom was on his feet and, with tear-wet cheeks, began witnessing the love of Jesus to Gary, just as if he had been doing it for years. I stepped back, raised my hands, and exclaimed,

"Thank you, Jesus! Praise Your Holy Name!"

I began to pray silently as Tom kept talking. When he finally stopped, he looked at me and then said to Gary,

"I don't know how I even knew what to say. The words just came out."

I then looked at Gary and asked,

"Are you ready to commit everything to Jesus?"

"Yes," he said, and we introduced him to our best friend, Jesus.

[On all our return visits Gary seemed to be feeling well, so I assume that he was healed that morning, though he gave no testimony to that.]

Though another brother had brought Tom, he wanted to go home with me so we left the jail and got into my car. Tom was on cloud nine, as even the car seemed to just float down the highway. He related to me what happened as I was praying for Gary.

"I knew," he said, "that I had to give everything I had or ever hoped to have to the Lord. I started out by giving my wife and children, my home and business, and then just completely submitted everything else to Jesus. Then I told Him that I would go anywhere and do anything He wanted me to do."

As he talked, I knew what had happened to him. It was the same thing that happens to so many of us who want everything that the Lord Himself wants for us. Though some may call it the "Infilling of the Spirit" and others may call it the "Baptism of the Spirit," what it is called is not the important thing; what is important is the powerful change that it can bring about in one's life, just as it had done in Tom's life.

That same afternoon when I went into his store, Tom was telling a young Christian couple what had happened that morning. In Mark, Chapter 8, we read that when Jesus first touched the blind man, the blind man saw only shadows, but when Jesus touched him the second time, he then saw clearly. So many of us need that "second touch" so that we, too, can see clearly. This is what happened to Tom, and, because of it, his whole outlook on the Christian Life had also changed. He began seeing people around him, whom he hadn't really seen in the "right light," as now needing Christ.

Tom later signed up to go with us in our motor home to a prison crusade near Waco, Texas. When the day finally came, we could all feel the excitement as we drove down the highway for the 26-hour drive to Waco. There were ten of us in our motor home, with three of them being first-time counselors. One of them was a young minister friend of ours named Sam. I can still picture these men sitting on the floor praying and praising the Lord in the middle of the night as we drove straight through all the way. We shared experiences, prayed, and discussed the Bible most of the time we were traveling. How it pays to pray diligently before arriving at these prisons! Our group of ten had over seventy decisions for Christ on that crusade! Once at the crusade, I noticed that Tom and Sam were like two honeybees in a flower garden going from "flower to flower" spreading the good news of the Gospel. Sam had led many persons to Christ prior to this Waco crusade, but this time it was a different side of life that he hadn't ever seen before. I remember how Sam exclaimed,

"Praise the Lord! All Christians should try this at least once—it would surely change their lives."

Sunday morning about 11:00 we said our tearful farewells to our friends at the prison. As we left, we looked back at the locked gates and could see the inmates waving goodbye to us. What an impression that leaves on the heart! Jesus really changed things for those inmates, and for us, too. There was singing, rejoicing, and crying all at the same time as we drove the two-hour stretch of road from Palestine, Texas back to our motel in Waco. At the motel, after we had everything loaded, we said our tearful goodbyes to the other counselor friends that we had made and thanked God for what He had done, both through us and in us. The ride home seemed shorter as we had so much to share. After being on the road for about an hour, we stopped at a fast-food steak house for a meal. As we went through the serving line, we found out that the checkout girl was a born again Christian, but we didn't get a chance to talk to the young man grilling the steaks behind the counter. After we finished our main course, Tom and I walked over to look at the desserts. At that time there were no other customers in the restaurant, other than our group. We then saw the young chef and the checkout girl talking to each other, so we walked over to them. I looked at the young man and said,

"I want to ask you something."

The girl enthusiastically urged me on, so I asked that young man the same question that I have asked scores of people—

"Do you know for certain that if you were to die today you would go to Heaven?"

Though unknown to us at that moment, because he had been doing just what the Bible says (seek and you shall find), a few minutes later he asked Christ to come into his life, which made the ride home filled with even more rejoicing.

Backtracking for a bit, the first important moment that I had at the prison was the very first hour I was out in the "yard area." Roger Staubach, the famous quarterback for the Dallas Cowboys, had just finished his testimony and football clinic with the inmates. We counselors were approaching the inmates for a time of "one-on-one" witnessing when I heard someone shouting my name. I spotted Pat, a young Christian inmate running across the yard toward me whom I had met two years earlier at another prison. After embracing for a few moments, the young man told me that he had been transferred to the facility here in Palestine because of his age. Two years previously, I had met Pat and another Christian named Mark at the Ferguson unit in Huntsville, Texas. At that time, we talked of Jesus in their dorm room and they both shared their love for Christ. Mark had said that he had a 99-year sentence, and Pat a 10-year term to serve. As we talked there in their dorm room two years prior, the Holy Spirit started to minister to me to pray for Mark to be released. In my thoughts I said to the Lord,"

Why not Pat since he has only ten years?"

But I had learned earlier in my Christian walk to obey the Lord, so I said to Mark

"The Lord wants us to pray for your release. I don't know how, but God is going to get you out, so let's pray and praise Him for it."

Now, here it was, two years later, and I found out that Mark was still in Huntsville and that Pat was here in Palestine, Texas. As a postscript insert, six weeks after we returned home I received a letter from Pat that said he had three miracles to tell me. First, his mother was saved while staying in a hospital; second, he was being released within the next thirty days; and third, Mark was on his way home! It seems that after five years, a judge had declared Mark's trial to be a "mistrial," and he was free to go home—and without any criminal record! God is so good! He wants to do so much for us if we will only ask and believe Him for it.

A few days after we were home, while I was doing some artwork, I was called out to the showroom, and there a tall, handsome man looked at me and said,

"Are you Bud?"

"Yes," I replied.

He grabbed my hand and said,

"I have just spent the last three hours with Tom and now I have Jesus in my heart!"

"Praise the Lord," I exclaimed.

He laughed and said,

"Tom said that you would say that!"

I couldn't help but think how different Tom had become. Tom had once told me how he previously thought that I carried my Christian life too far—that I was a fanatic.

"Now," Tom says, "I'm a fanatic just like you—and it feels good!"

We were to go to another crusade in South Carolina and Tom signed up for this one early. However, about two weeks before the crusade my wife walked into the hardware store and Tom took her aside and confided,

"Gertrude, I've got to go to the hospital. I found a large lump under my arm, so I went right to the doctor and he is operating on me in two days. Please pray for me."

When Gertrude related this to me, I immediately went to see him and prayed for him.

Tom said,

"If this would have happened before my experience at the county jail, I don't think I could have handled it, but now I have no fear—even if it is cancer."

Well, it was cancer. Right after the operation Sam and I went to see Tom and prayed for a complete healing. As it turned out, Tom had been advised to take radiation treatments and so different volunteers took him to Toledo for those. I took him for a particular treatment and he told me that his hair was starting to come out in small handfuls. I told him that we should ask the Lord to stop the hair from falling out, but he said that he would be happy just to be healed. He wanted to stop for a sandwich and when I asked the Lord to bless our food, I also asked for the Lord to stop Tom's hair from falling out—and you know, He did! It stopped falling out and started growing back, even with continued radiation treatments! One day Tom asked the doctor what the treatment did and he told him that it kills the bad blood cells.

"Doesn't it also kill the good blood cells, doctor?" Tom inquired.

"Yes," the doctor replied.

Tom told the doctor that he needed all the good cells he had, so he said to the doctor,

"I'm going to stop my treatments."

Now I'm not suggesting that anyone should do this; I'm just saying that is what Tom decided to do. At this writing, Tom has been cancer-free for more than 25 years because of the touch of God on his body.

In spite of his illness, Tom told us that he had already been sharing Jesus with others and that he still planned on going to South Carolina to the prison crusade, which was only a week away—and he did. We returned from South Carolina early on a Monday morning and that night Tom came to see me.

> "Bud," he said, "I have something to tell you. I had a dream about two weeks ago. I was riding in a school bus and talking to an old man about Jesus. I had my Four Spiritual Laws booklet and was going through it with him. When it came to the sinner's prayer part, he said that he wasn't ready to make a decision. Then, the bus backed up to a frozen pond and, when the door was opened, the old man got out and slipped down the icy bank onto the ice that covered the pond. What do you make of this?"

"Tom, you surely have a burden for the lost souls of this world," I replied.

"That's just what my pastor told me," Tom responded.

He continued,

"This afternoon as I was working in my store, I saw a customer come in the front door. I stood with amazement, almost frozen myself, as I looked into the face of the old man whom I had seen in my dream. I stood motionless as he walked past me and went back to the lawn mower department."

As I listened to Tom, I wondered how I would have reacted if this same thing had happened to me. Those "Holy Spirit bumps" were completely covering my body as Tom spoke. He told me how it took him a few minutes to get himself together, but that he followed the man back to the mower department, watched him make his purchase, and then followed him out the side door.

"Mister," Tom said, "I want to tell you something."

At this, the old man stopped and turned around. Tom proceeded to relate to me that he told the old man that he had had a dream about him and wanted to talk to him about it. The old man looked startled as Tom began to relate the dream to him.

"When I reached the part of my dream about the *Four Spiritual Laws* booklet, I actually took one out of my pocket as we were standing there, making it a reality."

The old man listened, and when he had finished, Tom's heart sank as the old man replied,

"I'm not ready for that yet," the exact response the man had given in Tom's dream.

Tom went back into the store as the old man walked down the street. As he never recalled seeing the man before, Tom asked one of his clerks who had worked there for many years if he knew the old man. The clerk replied that he knew him and also knew where he lived. A few nights later, Tom drove down an old country road to find Joe, the old man. Tom knocked at the door, and Joe invited him in. Tom said that he talked with the man for some time, but since he couldn't seem to keep him interested in spiritual things, he left.

About two weeks later, I was in Tom's store and we decided that the two of us would go out to see Joe the next night. We found Joe at home with his six dogs running all over the house. Joe sat in his chair with a loaded rifle within arm's reach and talked of how he would like to use it on certain people. I just listened quietly as he and Tom talked. Somehow, the subject of Joe's feet came up in the conversation, as he had bone spurs that hurt him when he would walk. Joe remarked that even Jesus couldn't heal bone spurs. With that, I jumped off my chair and sat by his feet amidst the six dogs and all the debris on the floor. Tom got down beside me and I asked Joe if we could pray for his feet, to which he consented. During the prayer, we rebuked the bitter spirit and asked the Holy Spirit to reveal the truth to Joe. When we finished the prayer, we asked Joe if he wanted to accept Christ into his life, to which he 'amazingly' responded, "Yes." After we left Joe, we stopped about two miles down the road where a Christian couple lived who agreed to follow-up with Joe. I have never seen Joe since that night, but several of our employees said that he had stopped by our trophy showroom a couple of times to see me, but that I was always out when he came. [We were so busy at that season of our lives, we thought it would be more productive for this Christian couple to follow-up with Joe.]

As for Tom, he has continued growing in his Christian life, going to prison crusades and giving his testimony of healing in many places. He also started a Bible Study at a boys' home for juvenile delinquents. All this is really just the beginning of Tom's story. God led him out of the hardware business a few years later, and he and his family moved to Florida where he attended a ministerial and pastoral school. Then, after serving as an associate pastor for some time at *Christian Retreat* in Bradenton, Florida, he was called by a church in Hampton, South Carolina to be their senior pastor. After serving there a few years, he started another congregation that held their Sunday morning and evening services at a skating rink facility, which the church eventually bought. They transformed the building into a church to serve for their Sunday services, as well as a Youth Outreach Center where one of Tom's sons became the youth pastor. The building now also has a Christian School. Tom indeed has a heart for the lost and those less fortunate. When we wintered in South Carolina for six years, on the day prior to Thanksgiving we would drive the hour over to Hampton to help his small congregation serve hundreds of free meals to those in need. A member of another denomination in Hampton, who always baked a turkey for the occasion, said that, "Tom is doing what Jesus intended the church to do."

Chapter 20
"Shopping in the Ladies' Department"

It was 1:45 AM and I had just gotten up from bed after lying awake for two hours, unable to sleep. I was talking to the Lord and He put on my mind that I should get up and write about an experience I had. This was the first time I had ever been instructed to get up and write something in the middle of the night.

A few days after Christmas, my wife and daughter decided that they wanted to go shopping in Toledo at some of those after-Christmas sales. Our family had given us a little money for Christmas so that we could buy some clothes that suited our personal tastes, which would not have to be returned. My thrifty wife said that the best time to shop is right after Christmas to get in on all the special sales that most department stores have, so the three of us left for one of Toledo's largest shopping centers. After dropping my wife and daughter off, I headed downtown to pick up some supplies for our business and returned in about an hour to find my wife and daughter in the ladies' department going through the racks of clothes on the floor. Now, going shopping with my wife in the ladies' department excites me about as much as shoveling snow on a day when it's freezing outside, but, once again, God had more meaningful plans for me.

I was standing in the middle of the ladies' department holding Gertrude's coat and watching my two girls search for bargains. I stood there shifting my weight from one foot to the other, hoping that they would quickly find the clothes they wanted. Believe it or not, things are much better than they used to be since Gertrude started asking the Lord to help her find the right clothes at the best price before she even goes shopping. She can get two different pieces of clothing at two different stores and they always match perfectly! Anyhow, I was standing there trying to figure out why God seemed to want me in the ladies' department when I noticed a young clerk hanging up clothes from a huge stack lying on the counter.

I enquired,

"Are all those clothes returns from Christmas?"

"Oh, yes," she said, "but this isn't anything to what we had Friday and Saturday."

She proceeded to tell me that she wouldn't have to work at this job much longer because she would soon be going back to college after Christmas break. She went on to say that she had received an engineering scholarship from the University of Florida. I pointed at our daughter over at one of the racks of clothes and told the clerk that we had spent Thanksgiving at *Oral Roberts University* in Tulsa, Oklahoma. I said,

"That is the most unusual campus I have ever been to because everyone there talks about Jesus and how much the Lord blesses them."

After I told her that our daughter was thinking of enrolling there, she quickly informed me that she had attended a parochial school during her high school years. She added,

"I'm not all that religious, but I don't go for some of the things I see going on in the world today."

Following her lead, I started telling her about Jesus and how He said, "You must be born again." I related to her how the prison counselors in the Bill Glass prison ministry are all from different denominations—protestant and catholic—but that they are all born again. Minutes flew by in no time and my feet weren't even tired! While I was talking, she suddenly stopped hanging up clothes, looked me right in the eye, and asked,

"How can I be born again?"

Power In Ordinary People

My heart leaped as I took out my Four Spiritual Laws tract and informed her that all the scripture verses in there could be found in her Catholic Bible. As I noticed her boss staring at us, I quickly explained to her the Four Spiritual Laws and pointed to the prayer in the tract that would show her how to be 'born again.' She thanked me a couple of times, but I told her to thank Jesus, as He was the One who would save her. She assured me several times that she was going to read it because she wanted to go to Heaven.

It was hard to leave a situation like that, but I felt that I had been led by the Holy Spririt. What a great time I had that day shopping in the Ladies' Department!

Our Wedding Day, August 4, 1946
Gertrude and Bud Hitt

Chapter 21
"Two New Births and a Motorcycle"

The last and final motorcycle I bought was from a man in Toledo who had advertised it in the paper. I called and made an appointment to see it, telling them that I would be there in about two hours. I was so excited about getting it that I asked them to please not sell it until I could see it. When I arrived there and saw that beautiful Silver Wing Interstate and the price, I knew that the Lord had something else in mind besides my just getting a good deal. Once I finalized the deal with the young man who was selling it, I took him along with me to the motor bureau where we had the title transferred into my name. In the meantime, our son-in-law Tom, whom I had taken along with me, drove the motorcycle back home. After the young man and I took care of all the title work, I took him back to his home and stayed awhile, talking to him and his mother about Jesus. A few minutes later they both received Jesus into their lives. Now <u>that</u> is what the Lord really had in mind for me that day! God is so good and He doesn't want anyone to perish, plus He also provided me with a motorcycle that I desired at a price that was in my budget. It's just like Psalm 37:4 says: "Delight yourself in the Lord and He <u>will</u> <u>give</u> <u>you</u> the desires of your heart."

The Bible says that we are to be ready to share Christ anywhere and anytime. Don't be afraid of being rejected because they aren't rejecting you but are instead rejecting Christ. Jesus confirmed this in Acts 9:4

when He spoke to Saul when Saul was persecuting the Christians. He said,

"Saul, Saul, why persecutest thou <u>me</u>?"

Though Saul was persecuting the Church, he was actually, and unknowingly, persecuting Christ Himself. Thus, we are only to give the message and then leave the rest in the hands of the Holy Spirit.

Our motorcycle days.

Chapter 22
"She's in a Coma!"

When our friend, Tom, was an associate pastor at *Christian Retreat* in Bradenton, Florida, he received a prayer request through their prayer line from a lady in Atlanta. She said that her daughter, Marsha, was in a coma at one of the Toledo hospitals and asked the phone counselor if there was anyone in the Toledo area that could go and pray for her. The lady calling in the request said that she worked as a receptionist and was sitting at her desk when she received the call about her daughter, and how, to her good fortune, sitting near her was another receptionist. Upon seeing how upset her friend was, the second receptionist asked her what was wrong. When she told her, her friend replied,

"I know of a place in Bradenton, Florida that has ministers all around the country. Perhaps they have one in the Toledo area who would go and pray for your daughter."

After the caller explained that was why she had contacted *Christian Retreat*, her request was referred to Tom, who then called us in Ohio. Once we knew the story, my wife and I made arrangements to visit the lady's daughter and headed to Toledo. When we arrived at the hospital, we asked for Marsha and were escorted to the intensive care unit where she was being kept. Her whole body was quite puffed up, which made her look heavy, and her skin had a noticeable yellow cast to it. Sensing that the nurse was a little nervous about us being there, we gently laid hands on Marsha and, in a very short prayer, asked for a miracle of healing in her body and then departed. At the time, which was a Sunday afternoon, we knew nothing as to exactly what was wrong with her. On the following Wednesday I needed to make a business-related trip to Toledo, so I decided to stop in and see Marsha at the hospital. When I got to her room, she seemed to be exactly as she was on Sunday afternoon when we first prayed for her, having the same yellow cast to her skin and just lying there. So, with a nurse looking on again, I simply laid my hand on her as I had before and said another short prayer. As I have said previously, the Bible tells us that God knows our needs before we even ask, but that He nevertheless is waiting for us to ask in faith. Given that assurance from God, we are to ask and leave the results up to Him.

The following Saturday Tom called me and asked,

"Have you heard about Marsha?"

I replied,

"We were down there on Sunday to pray for her and then again on Wednesday."

Tom said,

"You don't know the update then. Her mother called me and said that Marsha came out of her coma on Wednesday night and that the hospital called it a miracle!"

I hadn't been told that, but I was so overjoyed on hearing it that on the following Monday when I had to deliver trophies in Toledo, I decided to go and meet Marsha. When I went to her room there were several nurses and a man outside of her door putting on gowns to go into her room. As Tom had told me that she was married, I said to the man,

"Are you Marsha's husband?"

He replied that he was.

I told him that I would come back in a few days, as I didn't want to interfere with his visit. He asked me who I was, so I just told him that I had been there several times to pray for Marsha. He said,

"Are you that man that came and prayed for her when she was in a coma?"

I said,

"Yes", and politely said that I would return with my wife another day.

As Gertrude's birthday was coming up in a couple of days, I had already planned to take her to *The Red Lobster* in Toledo, one of her favorite restaurants, and I thought that occasion would be a good time to go and visit Marsha. As Marsha had been moved out of intensive care and into a standard room, when we walked into her room there was this small, pretty, young lady sitting up in bed. It was Marsha! Her husband, whom I had met briefly a few days earlier, was sitting there by her bed. After introductions, we were anxious to hear her story of recovery.

Apparently something had gone wrong in her pregnancy and she was in the last stages of toxemia, so the doctors did an emergency C-section and delivered a very small premature baby girl weighing a little more than two pounds. This was the first we knew that a baby was involved, and were later told that only 10% of such women ever survive that particular stage of toxemia that Marsha was in. As we talked to them, we carefully informed Marsha and her husband that it was not us who had healed Marsha but rather the power of God in the name of His Son, Jesus. The toxemia had puffed up her body and face to the degree that it had begun slanting her eyes. You would never think that this slim, no longer yellow, lady was the same person! More important than her physical healing was the spiritual healing that they both received that day. When we asked Marsha that, if she *had* died, would she have known for sure that she would have gone to Heaven, they both accepted Christ without any hesitation. After they had both prayed to accept the Lord, she then very sincerely asked us to pray for her newborn baby. Though it had survived the advanced stage of her mother's toxicity, it had been born with a hole in its little heart. Due to Marsha's severe medical condition, to save her life the doctors felt they had to perform a complete hysterectomy after delivering the baby. Thus, this would be their only natural child.

I then said,

"You are now children of God, the same as we are, so let's hold hands and agree together for God to heal your baby's heart."

Once again we just prayed a simple prayer asking God to heal their baby in the Name of Jesus. Then we went to *Red Lobster* praising the Lord for their salvation and Marsha's healing. Gertrude said that their salvation was the best birthday present she could ever have.

We returned to visit Marsha a few days later. As we greeted her, she said that she had great news! When the doctors checked the baby's heart, the hole was completely gone! No operation was even needed! Isn't God good? [Yes!!] We kept in contact by phone and when the little girl was a few years older Marsha and her husband invited us to their home for an evening meal and fellowship. Marsha told us that her husband was being transferred to another state, so that was the last contact we had with them. We kept Pastor Tom updated on all this and when we later went to *Christian Retreat* to winter for a few months, we called Marsha's mother in Atlanta on our way home. She was elated to hear from us and insisted that we stop by, have dinner with them, and spend the night. This, too, was God's plan because we also had the privilege of leading her to the Lord. We can only say, "Praise the Lord!"

Chapter 23
"The Unforgettable Trip"

When our youngest daughter, Candy, asked if she could spend three weeks at a music camp at West Virginia University, it sounded like a good opportunity for us to take a combination business trip and vacation because, only the week before, I had received an inquiry about my trophy business from the *Christian Broadcasting Network* (CBN) at Virginia Beach, Virginia, parent organization of the *700 Club*. We decided to take Candy to the university and invited two of our friends, Herb and Betty, to go along for our vacation time. The day before we left, the weather was muggy and one of those thunderstorms that often accompany such conditions left our office and showroom carpets soaked after a flash flood, but we soon had the mess cleaned up and our motor home ready to leave the next morning at 7:30 A.M. Thankfully, the Lord provided perfect weather for the trip. For our inside environment, we had worship music and sermons via the tape deck in the motor home, as well as Bible studies. We arrived at West Virginia University about 2:00 P.M. that day and, after taking Candy and her luggage to the dorm and saying our goodbyes, the four of us were on our way to Virginia Beach. Because we had no particular schedule, we just stopped whenever we wanted. As we were driving along, we saw a roadside sign that said REACT, and, from that, understood that coffee was being served at the next rest area. Though we had brought our own coffee, God had plans for us to stop.

On the side of our motor home I had painted "**THE GOSPEL HITS**" in bold letters, as that is the name we had selected for our family singing group (our last name being Hitt). In choosing that name, and displaying it on our motor home, our hope was that it would draw attention and open opportunities for us to share the Gospel. So, feeling prompted to pull off the road, even though we didn't really need any coffee, we drove into the rest area. While we were parked there, five young Christian men who were traveling down the other side of the highway spotted our singing group name on the motor home and turned around to come back to the rest area. As they got out of their vehicle and approached us, they started talking about the Lord. What a thrill it was to hear young people so turned on for Jesus. While we were talking, the Holy Spirit gave me (Bud) a Word of Knowledge about one of the young men. I turned to him and said,

"Within 24 hours you are going to meet someone who needs to know Jesus, and you must share the Gospel with him. The Lord does not want you to keep turning away from the opportunities that he has been giving you. From now on you must start sharing Jesus with a new boldness that He will give you. He also will give you the words to say. You will recognize the person we are talking about the moment that you see him."

As the young man was rejoicing over that, one of the other men said to me,

"I need your prayers because I have been in jail and now I'm out on bond until my case comes up for trial."

He explained to us that he had been accused of being involved in a "hired for murder" contract. He gave us some background of the incident, and said that he really did love Jesus, so I came right out and asked him if he was innocent of the crime of which he had been accused. His answer convinced me that he was, and his conduct and conversation indicated to me that he was sincere about serving the Lord, so I said

"Let's all pray in agreement right now for this situation."

We all held hands and everyone in the circle prayed.

The people who were serving the coffee were watching us, so I asked Herb to give each of them a *Four Spiritual Laws* tract, which is a four-step method explaining the Gospel and the plan of salvation. We said goodbye to the young men and headed back to our motor home.

As we turned, we heard the REACT group telling us goodbye, and they all had big smiles on their faces. We knew that we had obeyed the Lord by stopping and sharing Jesus, and so down the highway we went once again, rejoicing and praising our Lord for how He uses those who obey Him. Farther down the road we saw a sign, "Flea Market Ahead" and, at Betty's request, we pulled over and stopped. We walked around looking at various things on display, and near the end of the line of display tables was a lady selling pictures of Christ. This gave us an opening to share our faith with her, and we always feel good about those opportunities.

Soon we were once again headed down the road listening to beautiful tapes about our Lord when we saw a couple walking away from their disabled car. Since the traffic was heavy on this last evening of the Fourth of July weekend, making it unusually difficult to ease off the highway, it took about two hundred yards for us to get over and come to a stop. We finally pulled over at a guard railing, but knew that this was what the Lord wanted us to do. The young couple came running toward us and jumped up into our motor home, all out of breath. Since I (Bud) was driving, Herb took the young man, Danny, to the back, while Brenda, Danny's wife, sat up front with Gertrude and Betty. Brenda asked if we could drop her and her husband off at Hagerstown, about 22 miles up ahead. I could see in the mirror that Herb was busy talking to Danny about the Lord. Brenda asked us where we were headed and we told her that we were going to Virginia Beach to the *700 Club*. She responded that she had watched that program several times and remarked how well her day had gone after she had seen those *700 Club* programs. This gave me the opportunity to ask,

"If you were to die right now, do you know for sure that you would go to Heaven?"

She replied that she wasn't, so I asked if she would like to have that knowledge. She said that she would, and that was all I needed to hear. Gertrude and Betty shared Jesus with her and showed her I John 5:13, which tells us that we can <u>know</u> that we have eternal life—not a "hope so" but a "know so!" I was praying all the while, and as we turned off the superhighway and started into Hagerstown, Brenda was praying the sinner's prayer while tears trickled down her cheeks.

We were low on gasoline and I had already passed two stations that had relatively good prices, so I asked Brenda exactly where they wanted off.

She said, "Anywhere in Hagerstown is OK."

I was rejoicing so much for Brenda's salvation that I passed several more gas stations, so I interrupted everyone and said,

"I just have to stop and get some gas."

Just then Betty said, "There's a station over by that mall."

As we drove over to it, we saw that it was in fact the lowest price yet, which is important when you have two large tanks to fill. There was also a phone booth there for the couple to call their relatives. Herb and Danny came up to the front, and we rejoiced with them because Danny had just rededicated his life to Christ. After we prayed with them, we gave them a Bible and a Bible Study guide and said our farewells.

When I started pumping gasoline, I had a chance to talk to another man who was there getting gas. He came up and asked me what "**THE GOSPEL HITS**" meant. I explained to him that it was the name of our family singing group and I gave him a *Four Spiritual Laws* tract. When he left, he thanked me and promised to read the little booklet carefully. We continued on down the road, and after driving for a while we stopped at a roadside park to eat and rest. When Herb and I got out to routinely check the generator on the back of the motor home, two clean-cut young men drove up and asked if we needed help. They said that they were from Canada and were on their way to Florida for a vacation. Our wives joined the conversation, and soon we were talking about the Lord. One man knew the Lord and the other one said that he wasn't quite ready to make that decision. Because Jesus does not force himself on anyone, we just had a pleasant time talking with these young men. Since it was late in the day, they decided to spend the night in their car. As we also stayed there for the night, the next morning we found a nice note on our windshield saying that they had left very early. We knew that we had the privilege of planting a seed that the Lord would later send someone to water.

Once we arrived in Virginia Beach, we again had the opportunity to share our faith at the campground at which we stayed. We visited the *700 Club* for a day and then left for Charlotte, North Carolina and the *PTL Club*. What a beautiful time we had with all the precious Christians around us. On several occasions, people came to our motor home asking for prayer and wanting to know more about Jesus. After four beautiful days of being blessed on the *PTL* grounds, we headed for home, playing Bible teaching tapes the entire way.

On Monday, my work was piled up in my designing room and one of those was a 'rush job' for the National Tractor Pulling Championship that required me to have a large rubber squeegee. I knew that a business friend of mine who lived in a neighboring town would have an extra one, so I drove the ten miles to his place of business. [About six months earlier, when he had visited our factory and trophy showroom, I had taken him outside and shown him our "Showroom on Wheels" and talked to him about the Lord, but he wasn't ready at that time to make a commitment.] When I arrived at his place of business that morning, Dave was on the phone, so I chatted with his partner, Daryl. I started to tell him about our recent trip to Virginia Beach when he surprised me by asking if we had visited the *700 Club*. After we talked about that experience for a while, Dave hung up the phone and joined us, and I could see that he was very interested in what we were talking about. After about 45 minutes of talking (and a little preaching), knowing I had to get back to work I just came right out and asked Daryl if he had invited Christ into his life. He promptly replied that he had done that, which really came as no surprise as I could see it in his face. I said to Daryl,

"I have talked with Dave before and I know how he stands with the Lord" (that he wasn't quite ready to make the commitment).

At that, Daryl opened a drawer, pulled out a Bible and an *Our Daily Bread* booklet, and said,

"Dave and I have been reading this."

I then turned to Dave and said,

"Dave, I will be praying for you today."

Before I could say anymore, Dave said

"Pray for me right now!"

We both moved quickly to him and Dave threw one arm around each of us as I prayed. After a short prayer I said,

"Dave, are you ready for Jesus?"

At that, he burst into a prayer and asked Jesus to come into his heart. When he finished praying, and while we were yet in that circle, I gently placed my hand on his head and asked the Holy Spirit to fill him. All at once Dave said,

"I'm falling! My legs won't stay up!"

We quickly grabbed him and held him up as the Holy Spirit had overcome him.

"Wow", he said, "I feel like a big load has been taken away."

Dave rejoiced with tears rolling down his cheeks as I told him that I had seen the Holy Spirit's power before, but this was the first time it had happened to anyone while I was praying for them. I praise God for allowing me to see this power—then, and many times since. I am also thankful for Daryl who was bold enough to ask his partner to read the Word with him. He sowed the seed, I came along and watered, but of course its God Who always gives the increase.

Chapter 24
"Rest Home Experiences"

Some time ago Gertrude and I had friends that we would visit at our local Rest Home. After visiting them, I would often look in on others there at the Home and talk with them. One occasion when I was visiting some of these other folks, I was speaking with a 92-year old lady when she asked if I believed that God healed people. I replied that I did. She told me that she watched a certain evangelist on television who prays for people's needs, and asked if I would pray for her teeth and gums because they hurt all the time, to which I happily agreed. I prayed a brief prayer for her, and then left.

The next time I visited her, she said that she had gotten relief from the pain. I kept visiting her but I never asked her about her spiritual life. Now that's a little unusual for me, but it was because I hadn't felt led to ask her that. About six weeks later, I was relaxing at home in my easy chair on a Sunday afternoon when that little voice in my head said,

"Go to the rest home; she is now ready to receive Jesus into her life."

When I got there, this 92-year-old lady asked Jesus to be her Savior.

As often happens when I'm at nursing homes, I ended up visiting another friend's room who also happened to be there. He had just been given a new roommate, whose name was Loli. In the past, Loli had been an assistant foreman on the *New York Central Railroad* for years. During the summer of 1943, several guys from our graduating class went to work on the railroad. One day we were tamping stones under the ties with very loud air tampers. The two foremen for the day were over on a speeder, a small tram-like cart for hauling workers that could be set off/on the tracks. At that point in the day, the supervisors were not watching for trains like they should have been, and neither were we because we were so busy working. Suddenly Loli got our attention and pointed to a high-speed passenger train that was bearing down on us. In desperation, we started pushing one another into the ditch to save ourselves from the train—we all got off the tracks just in time as it flew by. The big jacks that we used to elevate the rails so we could put new stone underneath were still in place, as we had time to save only ourselves. To this day no one can explain why not even one of those heavy 24-inch-high jacks came loose under the weight of that fast-moving train, but I know that it was because of the Hand of God. The miracle was that, if they had come loose, they would have flown like shrapnel and been just another source of potential injury for us. So, as I was at his bedside at the Rest Home, I said,

"Loli, you saved my life many years ago and now I am here to show you how your life can be saved."

As my friend and his wife were silently praying, Loli became a new creation in Christ. Isn't it amazing how God works these things out in our walk with Him? Gertrude and I had the privilege of introducing a number of people at the Rest Home to Jesus and we had several more wonderful things happen there, but that's another story. Several years later God led us into another ministry, as our life seems to go from chapter to chapter.

Another story was when one of the older nurses at the Rest Home, who was a member of our church, asked if I would visit a particular woman who had a great fear of dying. As it turned out, this woman had been my eighth grade homeroom teacher and I remember that she asked us every Monday morning if we had been to Sunday School the day before. I didn't grow up in a family that went to church, and I went to Sunday School only a few times. I remember how happy I was that, on those rare occasions when I did, I could proudly raise my hand. This lady had also been a Sunday School teacher and was sincerely concerned that her students went to Sunday School. That is why I was quite surprised that she had such a fear of dying.

When I went to her room, I started quoting some scriptures that I thought she might remember to make her feel more certain that she could have the assurance that she would be go to Heaven if she died. I also went through the plan of salvation with her. At this stage of her life she could hardly speak audibly, but I tried to make sure that she was listening and then I went through a prayer with her. Although she couldn't speak, I could tell that she understood. Later on, the nurse who had asked me to visit her said that my former teacher was now much more relaxed and no longer afraid to die. It wasn't much later that she went home to be with the Lord. I often wondered why God picked me to minister to her, instead of one of the many other Christians who had been in our class. For whatever reason, God chose to use a former non-Christian boy from her eighth grade class. I cannot tell you how happy this made me.

Gertrude & Bud Hitt

Chapter 25
"Sore Neck Healed"

One time while traveling in Florida with our motor home, we stopped at a gas station in Lakeland for fuel. As I was pumping gas into the slow-filling back tank, Gertrude decided to walk inside the station. As she was walking out, two men approached her and asked if they could wash her car. She smiled and said that we weren't driving a car, but that we did have a motor home. They said that they would wash it. Gertrude told them that it really didn't need to be washed, but that she would ask her husband. When she came and told me what the men had said, I told her that I had washed it just before we left and it didn't need washed again so soon. She went back and told the men what I had said, to which they responded,

"Make us an offer!"

As I thought it would stop them from pestering us, I just told her to tell them $5.00, but, to our surprise, they said they would still do it! When I finished filling the gas tank, Gertrude went in to pay while I drove over to where they were washing cars. As I got out and walked around to the other side of our motor home, I could see a young lady just ahead of me who was slowly getting out of her car. Because she had her car door open in front of me, I just waited for her to swing herself out. In those moments, the Holy Spirit directed me to ask her a very personal question:

"Is there something wrong with your neck?"

She replied,

"Yes, it has been sore for three days and I'm on my way to the doctor."

This all happened so quickly that I didn't have time to fret about asking a total stranger about her neck. I told her that while going to the doctor was a good idea,

"I would first ask Jesus to touch me, if I were you."

At that she stepped forward and allowed me to pray for her. After a short prayer, I asked her if she wanted Jesus in her life, and she answered,

"Yes!"

I introduced her to my Lord just as Gertrude returned from paying for the gasoline, and then introduced my wife to this brand new Christian. Immediately Gertrude went into the motor home and retrieved some literature to help this new convert grow in the Lord.

When I walked over to pay the men for washing the motor home, I told them that the young lady had just given her life to the Lord. To that, one of the men said,

"That's my daughter!"

Gertrude and I then got into the motor home and were about to leave when the young lady came over, knocked on Gertrude's window, and said,

"Who are you people?"

She had not only been healed spiritually, but physically as well, because she said that all the neck pain had left her and that she finally felt that she was "back to normal." Gertrude simply told her that it really didn't matter who we were because it was Jesus who had healed her, and that He is the only One who matters. We drove off, never to see her again in this life, but we praise God that we followed the leading of the Holy Spirit and allowed those men to wash our motor home.

Chapter 26
"Sixteen Inches From Heaven"

A sobering thought is that nearly every prostitute, drunkard, convict, church member, non-church member, etc., in the United States knows about Jesus Christ. I make that statement because almost every person with whom I have shared the love of Christ has either been a present or past church member. Indeed, I have found that most have at least been in a church of some kind when they were young, and have had some exposure to Christianity. I am, in part, an exception, for though I had some rudimentary knowledge of who Jesus Christ was supposed to be, I was not raised in the church as a boy nor did we even have a Bible in our home. Rather, impressed upon my childhood memories were the "Good Friday" messages that were annually presented in the high school auditorium. Unfortunately, Good Friday services in schools are virtually nonexistent these days, except perhaps in some parochial schools. However, with such a multitude of television and radio ministries, this country and most of the inhabited world are hearing about Jesus, but being left @ sixteen inches away from Heaven (the approximate distance between the head and the heart). Nearly everyone knows in his/her mind who Christ is and/or who Christians say He is. It would be a shame, and an actual damnation, if you were to stand before God (which we all will eventually) and He said to you,

"Sorry, but I can't let you in. You left yourself just sixteen inches short of Heaven."

The following story is a sample of such a situation.

On the way to a men's prison crusade in Atlanta with my wife and our youngest daughter, we had planned to take a vacation to the East Coast right after the crusade. Because Gertrude doesn't drive our motor home when it's just the three of us traveling, I do all the driving. We had set our goal for the first day's travel to reach Chattanooga so that we could eat at a certain restaurant we knew of there. Everything went according to schedule and we arrived in Chattanooga in time for the evening meal. The restaurant had a very large parking lot, so we asked for and received permission to park there all night. In the morning, when I turned on the generator to shave, the TV also came on as we apparently hadn't shut it off the night before. As I walked out of the bathroom, an advertisement came over the TV about a local sale on the exact kind of car for which we had been shopping. Even though it was a 50-mile detour, we decided that we had the time to go and look at it. Having no problem finding the place of business, we parked our motor home across the street and walked over to the car lot. As all good salesmen, one came out immediately to greet us and to show us all of his "best bargains." He had shown us just about all the ones we were interested in when I pointed to our motor home across the street and said,

"That's what we're traveling in. We're on our way to a prison."

Needless to say, this stirred his curiosity. So I said to him,

"If you were to die right now, do you know for sure that you would go to Heaven?"

He answered that he thought he would; however, I came back with a second question:

"If you were to stand in front of God right now and He were to say, 'Why should I let you into my Heaven, what would you tell Him?'"

His answer was a typical one—he told me that he belonged to a certain church, that he helped in the church, that he tried to do good, etc.

> "These are the kinds of things a real Christian should do," I told him, "but they do not make one a Christian." (I always praise the Lord when I hear how someone is working in a church, but works never saved anyone.)

I continued,

"Those things are very good, but I have something that I would like to show you."

I then proceeded to show him what the Bible says a real Christian is, and went through the *Four Spiritual Laws* booklet with him. After doing that, I asked if he would like to ask Christ to come into his heart, and right there, over the hood of a used car in a little Georgia town, another child of the King was born. The message of the Gospel had reached sixteen inches lower into his heart.

Chapter 27
"Hawaii"

It finally happened! After years of looking for an excuse to spend the money to go to Hawaii, we signed up to be counselors for a Bill Glass prison crusade, as well as a City-Wide Bill Glass crusade during the same week, in Waikiki on Oahu, Hawaii. We decided to make our own reservations and stay two weeks instead of only one. We also thought that after the two crusades were over, we might be able to meet Pablo, who was the archery champion of Hawaii, since he shot our very own "HIT" bows to hunt and target shoot. Pablo had written us several times inviting us to visit him, but with our busy schedule and limited funds we didn't think it was really feasible. When we finally decided to make the trip, we didn't tell him ahead of time that we were coming to Hawaii, thinking that we would just obtain his phone number from the local telephone book when we got there and surprise him. As it turned out, since he was getting famous via the articles and photos of him lauding his hunting skills and feats in various archery magazines, Pablo had an unlisted number.

We got off the plane in beautiful Hawaii and that night the counselors met at a hotel for dinner and a briefing for the next day's crusade. I was telling some of the other counselors about our disappointment in not being able to reach Pablo when a local minister overheard my conversation. He asked us what Pablo's full name was, left the table for about ten minutes, and returned with Pablo's phone number! I didn't ask how he got it, but just thanked him. I then went to the phone, called the number, and Pablo answered. We were both excited. Pablo could hardly believe that we were in Hawaii, and frankly it was hard for us to believe, too. Immediately he invited us to visit him and see where he worked, which was for Dole Pineapple on the Island of Lanai. We were staying at Waikiki Beach, which is adjacent to Honolulu, so we had to purchase tickets on a small six-passenger airplane that did inter-island flights. We made arrangements with Pablo to fly to Lanai after the Crusade during our second week of personal time.

Ron Patty (father of Sandi Patty) and I were Bill Glass group leaders for the local holding center where inmates were held until their trial. Ron was not only a talented professional singer, but would fascinate the inmates with his softball fast-pitch demonstrations. Gertrude and another lady were counselors for one of the ladies' units. One of the inmates told her that she and the other ladies couldn't have come at a better time because there was apparently a lot of unrest within that particular women's unit. There were even rumblings that there might be big trouble between the different "gangs" there. Later that night, after spending the day in the unit, Gertrude related to her leader what she had been told and that there was now a sense of peace in that unit. The leader responded,

"We knew of the trouble brewing in that unit. Why do you think we sent you?"

As Gertrude was one of the more experienced counselors, they seemed to recognize that she went in to those situations clothed with the full armor of God. [Chapter 15 related Gertrude's encounter with a demon-possessed woman in a Texas prison.]

On the Monday following the crusades, we boarded a small plane to fly to Lanai, which at that time was exclusively a pineapple plantation owned by Dole. We always pray before flying and, as we taxied out on the big runway, the plane we were in must have looked like an ant beside those jumbo 747s. Once clearance was granted, the pilot revved up the engines for takeoff, but the left engine sounded like it had a wrench in it. Recognizing that something wasn't right, the pilot called the tower and told them that the plane had mechanical problems and that he would be returning to the terminal. My wife and I knew that God was in control to make the problem known before we were in the air, because it could have happened over the water had we taken off.

As soon as another plane became available, we again thanked God in advance for a safe trip and landed safely at a tiny runway on Lanai. As we got off the plane, we saw a young woman sitting at a card table watching the construction of an office building on that site that looked to be the size of a double-car garage. Pablo was anxiously awaiting our arrival, and we finally met each other face-to-face for the first time. He was driving a 1941 World War II Jeep that he had refurbished so well it sounded and looked like new. On arriving at his small humble home, we met his wife Loraine who brought out some fur-lined flight jackets and handed them to us.

I said,

"What do we need these for? It's 82 degrees outside?"

Pablo is a Philippino but, in broken English, said,

"You need 'em, you need 'em!"

We climbed into their Jeep and within 20 minutes were high in the mountains where we were more than happy to be wearing those fur-lined jackets! Pablo showed us where he bow-hunted for goats and other animals. He was very familiar with that mountainous area, so much so that he was generally the first one that rescue workers would lower down from a helicopter when a mountain climber would get in trouble. We then headed down to the pineapple fields where he cut open a ripe pineapple for us. We have never eaten such delicious sweet fruit! He said if he had known ahead of time that we were coming, he would have had a case of them ready for us to take back to the States. [We were sorry we hadn't notified him!] Then he took us to a beautiful, secluded, white sandy beach where there weren't more than ten people. The weather is generally so perfect on Lanai that Pablo kept a year-round vegetable garden there that he harvested and then gave the fresh vegetables to seniors. Pablo, Loraine, and I sat on a log watching Gertrude wading at the edge of that beautiful "Blue Hawaii" water. I said to Pablo and his wife,

"Living in this place of beauty is the nearest thing to Paradise, but, even with all this, do you know for sure that if you were to die right now you would go to Heaven?"

Pablo started to justify my question with an answer when his wife interrupted him and said,

"Pablo, let him talk."

By now Gertrude was at my side, silently praying as I presented the plan of salvation to them, after which they both prayed to receive Christ as their Savior. We all rejoiced over two new believers coming to Christ.

As Pablo was a shipping foreman, he took us to see where the bigger ships came to his little island and picked up all the pineapples, which they then took to one of the larger islands for processing. [Lanai is only about five miles wide and seventeen miles long.] I understand that Dole has sold that acreage and it is now a large resort area with hotels and golf courses, instead of an old town with about 2500 workers enjoying the quietness of their paradise. Pablo's wife said that he liked to stay up late and listen to the PTL club, particularly the music. No matter what we think, God has a way of using all of His children, if they are just willing to speak for Him. After a perfect day, the plane landed at 5:00 P.M. for our return trip. As we were about to board, Pablo embraced me and whispered in my ear,

"Now tonight I can sleep!"

I took this to mean that the Holy Spirit had been wooing him, perhaps by listening to the PTL programs, so that we could then lead him to the peace and assurance of salvation on that day.

We did a number of interesting things with some of the other counselors for part of that second week. We went on a dinner cruise with our friend, Nick the Greek, a former prisoner, who now has a prison ministry called, *INSIDE OUT*. Perhaps you have read his book, *Too mean to Die*. A fun activity was when Nick took me to *Diamond Head* on the back of a rented motorcycle. That was really a thrill, or should I say "a scare." As we still had a few days to ourselves after the rest of the group left, someone told us about a good restaurant across the street from where we were staying (the Outrigger West Hotel in Waikiki), so we decided to go there for our evening meal. As we walked into the lobby, there was a senior gentleman playing songs from the 30's, 40's, and 50's on an old upright piano. After having heard only Hawaiian music for the past few days, it was a nice change for us. Sitting on a stool with her cheek on her hand and elbow resting on top of the piano was a lady who also seemed to be enjoying that kind of music. After we had eaten and paid for our meal, we walked through the lobby where the man was still playing and the lady was still listening. Gertrude stopped and asked,

"Could you play our love song from our courtship days?"

She told him that it was *How Deep Is The Ocean*. He answered,

"Lady, I'll play it if you sing it."

Little did he know that he was talking to a singer that had had a restaurant for thirteen years with a jukebox that was always playing something. He started playing *"How Deep is the Ocean"* and Gertrude started singing! When she finished, to our surprise the audience began asking for more requests. I knew that she would stay there as long as they kept asking, so after seven or eight songs I finally said,

"Lets go to our hotel."

When we left, the lady who had been leaning on the piano walked across the street with us, since she happened to be staying at the same hotel. As we went up the elevator, Gertrude wanted to stop at one of the intermediate floors to browse the shops there, but the lady and I remained on the elevator. When the elevator stopped at her floor, I handed her a *Four Spiritual Laws* booklet and asked her to read it, which she politely took from me.

On another night, as I was walking from the hotel to purchase some carryout chicken for Gertrude and me, I heard a girl say something to me but wasn't quite sure what she said. It sounded like she had said,

"Do you want a date?" but I thought I must have misunderstood and went on. Then another young girl approached me and asked,

"Are you lonely?"

Then I realized that they were prostitutes trying to solicit a 57-year-old man. I quickly replied,

"No, I'm not lonely—I have Jesus."

At that reply, she quickly walked away. However, when I returned with the chicken carryout, I saw that same lady, who asked me if I was lonely, come out of *The International Market* there. She looked at me, then looked down, and shyly said,

"I'm still at it," and quickly walked away. How sad I felt for her.

Another time we led some young men in a restaurant to the Lord. On other occasions, we merely sowed the Gospel seed into hearts for others to water at some later time. Previously I had spoken about Jesus a couple of times with a lady who ran one of the hotel gift shops, who was a Buddhist. She told us that her son had gone to the States and had become a Christian, though she was not ready to make that commitment yet. When it came time for us to leave for the airport, I felt led to talk to her again. I told her that we were leaving and wanted to say goodbye, and then said,

"I thought I would ask you one more time if you want to accept Jesus into your life, just as your son has done?"

Praise the Lord, she said, "Yes," and so I led her in a prayer of conversion.

We took our luggage out to the taxi and headed for the airport where there was a long line waiting for seat assignments. Since it was an economy flight, and there were nearly 400 people on that plane, everyone had to wait. We had just gotten in line when a lady from the airlines came up to us and said,

"The woman at the counter has your seat assignments taken care of."

At the time, we had no idea just how that happened but it turned out to be through the lady who had been leaning on the piano enjoying the old music the night before, whose name was Marie. The three of us were assigned to seats in the same row. We thanked her and introduced ourselves to Marie, who happened to be a lawyer for a well-known organization. Due to a heart attack, she had lost her husband who had been one of the physicists that helped put our astronauts on the moon. She said that their friends had drifted away after she lost him and didn't invite her to their parties or functions anymore. At that point the flight attendant served us our colas, and Marie her small bottle of wine, after which they served us our meals. When we had finished eating, Marie asked the attendant for another bottle of wine and, after drinking it, she said,

"I think I'll take a nap."

Gertrude said,

"Before you do, do you know for sure that if you were to die right now that you would go to heaven?"

"No," she answered, "I would go straight to Hell."

Gertrude said,

"You don't need to!"

She went on to explain the plan of salvation to her, and Marie accepted Christ. When we landed in Los Angeles to change planes, there was someone waiting for Marie. To our good fortune, she asked them to drive Gertrude and me to the boarding gate where our plane to Chicago was docked. If they hadn't, we would have missed our flight because we arrived there just in time for boarding. Once again God was looking out for us every step of the way.

Gertrude and Bud back home after a Bill Glass Prison Crusade in Hawaii.

Chapter 28
"My Correctional Experiences"

The first few years that we went to *Christian Retreat* in Florida we had a motor home that we would stay in for the three-month time we generally spent there. One year, our friend Tom, one of the assistant pastors at *Christian Retreat*, asked if we would go to the local jail in downtown Bradenton to give the Sunday morning service. We of course agreed. Once we arrived there, Tom introduced us to the chaplain and then the inmates were brought in. We started the service with Gertrude playing her Omnichord and leading the songs. As the service progressed, Tom and the chaplain seated themselves toward the back of the room. While I was commenting on the Bible passage that I had selected, I suddenly stopped and asked Gertrude to stand up. I said,

"It doesn't take much of a man to beat up on a woman. I could break every bone in my wife's face with one good blow." I then added, *"I don't know why I said that, but maybe some of you here abuse your wives—don't do that."*

At the time, I noticed that Tom and the chaplain looked at each other rather strangely. I continued my teaching, but couldn't help but wonder why I had stopped and made those particular comments. Brushing it all aside, I finished my sermon, gave the inmates a chance to receive Christ, and then proceeded to pray for them. A tall man, approximately six-foot-six, came forward for prayer along with several others. We prayed for all of them and then closed the service, after which the inmates were ushered back to their cells. You could hear them singing as they went down the hall, *The Joy of the Lord is my Strength*, the song that Gertrude had just taught them.

Tom approached me and said,

"Do you know why you stopped in the middle of your sermon and made the comments about the broken bones?"

"No," I replied, "It startled me when I did it."
Tom responded,
"That tall fellow who came forward for prayer is in here for breaking all the bones in his wife's face."

Sometimes following the leading of the Holy Spirit doesn't seem to make sense at the time, but eventually the reason is revealed. You may even blurt out something and wonder why you even said it, but the Lord has a reason if you are under His control.

Another example of that happened at our old county jail in Wauseon located about ten miles from our home, which has since been demolished. A large five county jail has been built which is nearer to us. The Gideon's, of which I am a member, generally visited the inmates at the old jail on Saturday mornings. One of the Gideon brothers came to me and said,

"There is a young man here for DUI and we just can't seem to get through to him. He said that he quit going to church because there are too many hypocrites in the church."

He then asked if I would go and talk to him. While walking to his cell, I was praying and asking the Lord to give me the right words to say.

As I looked into the cell I said,

"They told me that you don't like hypocrites, but I wouldn't be surprised that you have sat in bars and gotten drunk with hypocrites. If you can't stand them, why would you want to go to hell and spend eternity with them?"

Power In Ordinary People

Those words got his attention, and in a few minutes he received Christ into his life.

The 14th, 15th, 16th, and 17th chapters of the Gospel of John contain some of my favorite verses in the Bible. There Jesus tells us that the Holy Spirit is our counselor and will be <u>with</u> us and <u>in</u> us to guide us into all truth. Sometimes we try to be too self-sufficient and not allow the Holy Spirit to guide us.

As we had made a decision to spend approximately six months of the winter at *Christian Retreat*, we purchased one side of a duplex so that we wouldn't have to stay in our motor home. The winter after we made that purchase, I began attending the Saturday morning Gideon meetings. There I met Billy, a Gideon brother, who headed up the jail ministry at a new 1600-unit correctional center at Port Manatee, Florida, about 30 minutes from *Christian Retreat*. The two of us decided to begin visiting this correctional center every Tuesday and Thursday evening. Gertrude would often go with us one of the evenings so that she could go into the women's unit there. In total, there were about 30 people from different churches who would go into designated areas/units. After the head chaplain learned of our many years of experience in prison ministry, he permitted me to go into one of the units alone to hold Bible studies on those two evenings. One of the first nights after starting that Bible Study, they put my little group in a separate room so that we wouldn't be disturbed. As was my custom, when I concluded the Bible study time I would then pray for the needs of the inmates who, one by one, would come and sit by me for prayer. Since we were all together in this room, everyone could hear what I was saying to each of the men, as well as what each of them would tell me.

During one of these evening sessions, a young man came and sat beside me for prayer whose name was Jimmy. At that time of his life, he had a full beard and exceptionally long hair. In the hearing of the other inmates, Jimmy began to tell me about his prayer needs. He said that he was facing two 7-year sentences for robbery, which I later read about in the local paper. When I asked Jimmy if he was married, he replied that he wasn't. He told us that his parents lived in another state and that he really had no one close to him. He had just drifted into town and didn't really know anyone except one girl, whom he knew only by her first name and then only well enough to say hello. He went on to say that since

Jesus had come into his life, he wanted me to pray that the judge would have mercy on him and lighten his two sentences. [We found out that he had been previously saved under someone else's influence in the jail ministry.] At that point, God began a supernatural thing. Since Jimmy and I were sitting there facing each other in front of the group, I reached out and took his hands because I believe a "point of contact" is important when I pray for people. As I started praying, and with my eyes closed, suddenly a picture of a young woman appeared before me in my mind's eye. I stopped praying, opened my eyes, and said to Jimmy, in the hearing of all the others,

"Jimmy, I know what that girl looks like that you told us about,"
and I proceeded to describe her. Somewhat amazed, Jimmy asked,
"How do you know her?"

I told him that I didn't really know her, but God had chosen to reveal her to me so that I could give him a message, at which point complete silence came over the entire room. I looked around and told them all that if what I was about to say did not come to pass, that would make me what the Bible calls a "false prophet" because it came from me and not from the Lord. But here is what the Lord told me to say:

"Tell Jimmy that this girl is going to come and visit him and that just before she leaves, she will say, "Jimmy, wherever they send you, I am going to come and visit you." So I told him.

Jimmy just sat there looking at me in disbelief, but then managed to say in a sort of questioning tone,
"But we hardly know each other."

When I went back the next week, it was Bible Study as usual, with one exception—Jimmy had shaved off his beard and gotten his hair cut! I could hardly believe that the handsome young man I was looking at was Jimmy. After the study, I had prayer as usual with the men, at which time God began to initiate another miracle. One of the inmates came forward and said that he wanted prayer for his back. The story was he had been in a car accident that had left him in constant pain, which required him to be on medication. So I laid my hands on his back, prayed a short prayer, and he went back to his seat. As I was praying for the next man who had come up, I noticed that the man for whom I had just prayed got up and left the room. Well, not much deters me so I just continued on as usual. The next week when I returned, I had a packed room of inmates and of course there was always someone new to pray for. After Bible Study, the man who had the bad back spoke up and said,

"Bud, did you see me leave last week after you prayed for me?"

"Yes", I said.

"Do you know why I left?" He continued.

I said that I didn't really know why he would get up and leave in the middle of our prayer time. As all the men sat there and listened expectantly, he told me that after I prayed for him, as he returned to go back to his seat, the pain seemed to disappear. He was so curious to know if he was really healed that he got up and left the room so he could go downstairs to "work out." He wanted to see if the pain would return, but it didn't! We all joined him in praising the Lord for his healing. He told us that when I had prayed for him the week before, it felt like an electrical shock had hit him (though I felt nothing). God did many other things to show those men that He is real, and that no matter what they had done in their past, He was ready to forgive them and answer their prayers.

When I came back the third week for what I thought would be just another routine Bible Study, the inmates were waiting at the door to escort me in. As we sat around the big table we used, they excitedly told me about the week's events. They said that a prison officer had come into the unit and announced to Jimmy that he had a visitor. As they had been present when I told Jimmy a few weeks earlier that he would get company, they asked the officer if it was a woman, to which he replied,

"Yes, it's a female."

They began to speculate as to who it could be. Could it really be the girl that Jimmy knew only by her first name? Could it be the same one that Bud said was going to visit him? Jimmy went out to see, and in an hour or so returned with a big smile on his face. They said that they rushed up to him and asked,

"Was it her Jimmy? Was it really her?"

"Yes." Jimmy said, "It was!"

He then told them that the last thing she said to him as he was being led back to the cell area was,

"Jimmy, wherever they send you I am going to come and visit you!"

No one is more amazed than I at seeing God do these wonderful things to strengthen our faith in Him. I do nothing on my own. I am simply an ordinary man trying to follow the leading of the Holy Spirit. I just try my best to live as the Bible says—"Everything that you do and say, do in the name of Jesus."

There is a footnote to the story because, after we returned to Ohio, I received a letter from Jimmy who had been transferred to a state prison. He said,

> *"Bud, that first night when you prayed for all the drug and alcohol addiction to leave my body, I want you to know I have lost all desire for them and have had no withdrawal of any kind. But you forgot to pray for my smoking."*

Gertrude and I got quite a chuckle over that, so I guess that he and the Lord will have to work that one out. I have one regret about this story and that is somehow I must have misplaced his letter and wasn't able to contact him again. However, I am sure that God sent another Christian into Jimmy's life to disciple him. [Under the Privacy Act, a prison is not permitted to give out forwarding addresses, so we were unable to trace the prison to which Jimmy had been transferred.]

After some years, we felt led by the Holy Spirit to sell our winter home at *Christian Retreat* and winter at Sun City Hilton Head in South Carolina. However, each year we would return to *Christian Retreat* for a breakfast gathering of people from our Ohio area and stay on site for several days. On one of those trips back to *Christian Retreat*, I decided I would go to the Port Manatee Correctional Center for one more visit. I wasn't sure that I would be permitted to go in, since I didn't have a valid counselor's pass on file anymore, but the chaplain agreed to let me in as long as someone who did have a permanent pass accompanied me. Finding such a man, we were allowed two hours in the unit. As it turned out, the man I went in with preached to them for one hour, but in a rather harsh and condemning way. Though I wanted to, I couldn't really say much because I was simply a guest. God must have known this because, to my surprise, the man turned to me and said,

"Would you like to take over and share with the fellows?"

Of course I said,

"Yes!"

I started teaching from Romans 8:1 where it says,

"There is therefore now no condemnation to those who are in Christ Jesus."

Suddenly I knew that I was to tell one of the men an unusual thing. I don't remember the exact words, but it went something like this. I said directly to this particular man, who was about forty years old and very clean cut,

> "I perceive that you are an employer and that you've been telling your employees what to do since you are the boss. I see you hurting someone that you care for by saying very bad things to him. I envision you being in a parking lot with this man and that you are using very foul language. After he left, you felt very bad but it was too late, as the words had been said."

He then proceeded to tell the whole group that what I said was correct. He in fact owned a large automobile agency and had made a costly financial blunder that landed him in jail. Knowing that he was in trouble, his pastor had come to visit him at his place of business. They met in the parking lot where he cursed his pastor and rudely told him to leave. This opened the way for me to pray for him and other inmates. I haven't any idea what this meant or how it impacted his life or the lives of the other inmates, but I am sure that God had a very good reason.

Chapter 29
"It Happened At Christian Retreat"

Marge, a 75-year-old lady from Canada, came to visit a friend in the Bradenton, Florida area. Since *Christian Retreat* had a telecast that reached Canada, which Marge had watched on occasion, she thought that she would come and visit. This was during the time Gertrude and I had a winter home on the *Christian Retreat* grounds and taught an evangelism class at the *Institute of Ministry* there.

Marge attended one of our classes and afterwards we invited her to attend the "Prayer and Share" meetings that were held Monday through Friday mornings. For the years that we wintered there, Gertrude and I led the Friday morning sessions. The general format was that everyone could share what was on his/her heart, after which we would then pray for anyone who desired prayer. Marge went the next morning and told how she happened to be there. She also shared how she had become crippled from a bad fall earlier in her life. The people at the meeting then laid hands on Marge's ankle and prayed. Though it happened to be a day when we were not there, the ones who were present said that her ankle "popped" and that she got up from the chair completely healed. Marge was just ecstatic and, although she had been a church member for years, realized that she didn't really know Jesus as Savior, at least not in His fullness. At 75 years of age, she was not only made whole physically that day, but spiritually as well.

Marge was a widow and came back every winter to *Christian Retreat*. We became good friends over those years. She kept in contact with us through letters, which often said how much she was looking forward to her wintering at *Christian Retreat*, reminiscing of the good times with the friends she had made there. Many of those friends also reserved their rooms there at the same time each year so they could all be together.

Marge's doctors could not understand where Marge got her energy, as she had had a bad heart for years. The time finally came when her two sons did not want her leaving Canada or doing much of her own work any longer, so they put her in a beautiful assisted living home. One year Gertrude and I decided to visit her, so we called ahead and told her we were coming. When we got there, she told us that she hadn't slept the whole night in anticipation of our being there with her. About a year after our visit, Marge went to be with Jesus. She is only one of the many wonderful friends that we met at *Christian Retreat*.

Another such couple was Ed and Helen from the St. Louis area. They, too, had heard of *Christian Retreat* so they drove down to Florida to check it out. On one visit, they sat through our 1-hour evangelism class, which ended at noon. We followed them to the cafeteria for lunch and ate with them. As we lunched, Ed told us that he had been a Catholic priest for 25 years in the St. Louis area, but that he had met a lady whom he wanted to marry, so he left the priesthood and married her. She later died, but then he met Helen, a widow, and they were married. After much mutual sharing together over that lunch, they decided to get a motel room and stay for a few more days.

The next day Ed approached us and asked me an unusual question.

"Do you have the credentials to baptize people and, if so, will your baptize us?"

I told him that although I had been ordained many years ago and had the credentials, I was only a guest speaker and not a formal *Christian Retreat* staff person. However, I told Ed that I would get my friend Tom, who was an associate pastor there, and together we would baptize the two of them.

The next day down at the Upper Manatee River, which flows through *Christian Retreat*, we had the baptism for Ed and Helen. A crowd had gathered on the riverbank to watch the baptism and, when Ed came up out of the water, his hands were raised high and he was singing very

Power In Ordinary People

loudly the little chorus "Alleluia." The next moment Helen came up out of the water with her hands raised, also singing "Alleluia." It was almost as if it had been scripted (but it wasn't). It was such a stirring event that the whole crowd turned into a choir and joined them in singing, which echoed down the river. We could feel God's hands guiding this whole occasion, as no human could have planned it any better.

A lady who was in the crowd asked if we would baptize her in the swimming pool, as she needed a cane to walk with and the river bank was a little slippery for her to safely navigate. Thus, we went from the river to the pool and, with others looking on, we baptized her. As she came <u>walking</u> out of the pool, she realized that she wasn't even using her cane! Yes, she was fully healed and no longer needed the cane to walk. But the story continues.

A couple that was watching all this from the motel balcony came down and asked Tom and me if we would baptize them. Of course we first made sure that they knew Jesus as their Savior. It turned out that they were traveling athletes who gave demonstrations and broke boards using their karate skill as a tool to evangelize. They said that while they had accepted Christ as Savior, they now realized that they needed to get baptized. Because Gertrude had asked the Lord who he wanted us to have lunch with that day after our class, had we not obeyed Him to join Ed and Helen at their table all of the foregoing might not have happened.

Our middle daughter, Penny, and her little girl, Krista, came to visit us at the *Retreat*. We had been asked to go to the Pittsburgh Pirates' training camp at Bradenton to share in giving a service there, so we took them along. The manager of a Pittsburgh Christian television station was there and asked the audience for anyone needing prayer to raise his or her hand. It was an eye opener to see the degree to which these young rookies' shoulders, arms, legs, and backs had gotten injured for which they needed prayer. After all those requesting prayer were prayed for, Penny told the Christian television owner the doctor had told her that Krista's eye, which wouldn't stop running, would have to be surgically repaired. The station owner laid his hands on Krista's eye and prayed a simple prayer for healing. Before Penny and Krista flew home the next day, she didn't really notice any difference in the eye. We told Penny not to lose faith and that we believed Krista would not have to have surgery. Three days later Penny was talking to a friend on the phone that asked about Krista's eye, when she suddenly realized she had not been constantly wiping her eye. She ran to look at Krista, and saw that her eye was not running! Krista had been healed and the problem has never come back. Penny waited two more days and then said to her husband,

"Have you noticed that our little girl's eye has been healed?"

Krista is now 21 years old.

These are just a few of the many wonderful things that took place while we were wintering at *Christian Retreat*.

Krista & Mama Penny
GOD healed her eye.

Chapter 30
"In A Heartbeat"

You know, God is interested in little things. Sometimes we think that we can't go to God and talk to Him about things unless they're really big and important. The Bible says that Jesus told us that we could ask the Father anything in His Name—anything (John 14:13). There's no limitation—small, medium, or large—it just says "<u>anything</u> in My Name…" As I had problems with a skipping heartbeat for almost two years, I had been to several doctors to see if they could isolate the problem. They examined me thoroughly and told me that the heart has four stages it goes through on every beat, and, because one of the four functions was irregular for my heart, that was why my heart was skipping. They checked my heart with all kinds of things, even going down my throat thinking that they could discern something in that way, but in the end, decided there wasn't much they could really do. It was very troublesome for me, and got to be quite a problem because I just couldn't get used to it. Though it wouldn't do it all the time, sometimes it would go on for hours, and when it lasted that long I wasn't sure whether my heart was going to stop beating or not. I had a lot of prayer over it, but nothing seemed to happen. However, I continued to expect the Lord to heal me. One day I was down at *Christian Retreat* in Florida trying to learn how to hit a golf ball. I had a golf cart I used on the grounds there and they had a large mowed area where I could practice hitting golf balls all I wanted. One morning about 8:00 I was out there by myself hitting golf balls and my heart started acting up again. Finally, I just said,

"Lord, I don't think I can handle this anymore, so I'm going to ask in the Name of Jesus, Father, that You just have mercy on me and heal this heart that keeps skipping."

It was only a simple sort of prayer, but in just a 'snap of the fingers' it was over and I have never been bothered since, and that's been more than 15 years ago.

Another incident that may seem like a little thing was when I was putting carpet in the motor home we owned at the time. I was crawling around on my hands and knees when suddenly my left knee snapped. It cracked almost as if someone was clapping his or her hands, or like a rifle shot. From that day forth I was bothered with that knee. It would pop in and out of position and would hurt, requiring me to be very careful of the way I turned it. One night about two years later, I was watching *The 700 Club* about 11:00 P.M., which is rare for me because I'm usually not awake that late. Ben Kinchlow was talking and he was just ready to go to prayer. All of a sudden, the Lord gave Ben a Word of Knowledge and he said,

"There's someone out there who has a knee that pops in and out and the Lord is healing it."

Since my wife was out in the kitchen and I was watching TV by myself, I jumped up and said,

"That's me! That's my knee that's going in and out!"

Remember that at 11:00 P.M., the segment I was watching was merely a rerun of the morning program. Though the program wasn't "live," the Word of God is! When I started walking around the room, my knee didn't pop in or out and I've never had that problem since. Again, God is interested in what you may think is something far too little to annoy Him with, but He isn't annoyed at all—He's just waiting to do things for us if we will only ask Him.

Chapter 31
"When Some Prayers Go Unanswered"

I cannot give an explanation as to the 'why and how' of God's timing, nor can I explain why some people are healed and others are not, but one thing I know is that God's Word is true. He tells us "By His stripes we are (were) healed" (Isaiah 53:5, I Peter 2:24). "And all things, whatsoever you shall ask in prayer, believing, you shall receive" (Matthew 21:22). Other healing scriptures are Mark 11:24, John 14:13,14, and John 16:23. These scriptures, along with many others in His Word, tell us that we are to come boldly to the Throne of Grace so that we may obtain mercy and find grace to help us in time of need (Hebrews 4:16). So, we come boldly to Him and simply <u>ask</u>—not demand. Mark 15:18 tells us that we are to lay hands on the sick and that they will recover. John 14:12 says, "Verily, verily, I say unto you, He that believeth on me, the works that I do shall he do also." Therefore we must be about our Father's business as Jesus was, and do what Jesus did, by reaching out to the needy, praying in faith to the Father in Jesus' Name—and then leave the results up to Him.

We believe in the skills of doctors and surgeons, and we should pray for them to have special wisdom, especially before surgery. Jesus was trying to teach perseverance when He told about the woman who kept coming to the unrighteous judge for her petition (Luke 18). After many times of coming to the judge and presenting her case, the judge finally granted it. Jesus goes on to tell in that parable, 'How much more will our Righteous Heavenly Father grant our requests when we persevere in faith?' We pray for each other's health all the time and then, if we don't get well, we go to the doctor. As far as praying for others, some use the excuse that "It might not be God's will" to pray for themselves or others, yet they still go to the doctor. The basic logic of that thinking is, if you don't feel it is God's will to be healed, then why even go to the doctor? We have raised three daughters and when they wanted something from mom or dad, they didn't consider if it was our will or not. They just asked and hoped that we would say "yes." They still ask and, whenever possible, we continue to say "yes." [Though our resources are limited at times, God's resources are not!] Because God sees the inside and man sees only the outside, this means that God already knows what is on our hearts and that He also knows our needs before we ask. Some will say, "Why ask if He already knows our needs?" Again, His Word says in James 4:2, "You have not because you ask not." We should not lose faith when the answer isn't what we want. Instead, we must remember that God is sovereign and always in control. We must continue to believe and persevere in our faith and our asking.

 A few years ago there were two 19-year-old young men from our area with the same first names who both happened to have the same blood disorder. A number of us prayed for both of them to be healed, yet, in spite of all the prayers, one of them died but the other was healed. He went into the ministry and is a pastor. Yet, in spite of the tragic death of the other young man, when we went to the funeral, we witnessed several of his young friends commit their lives to the Lord. Could that have been the higher, more eternal purpose of his dying, while God allowed the other to live? We of course don't know; only God does. Two other very dear neighborhood men have gone to be with the Lord as the result of cancer, even though many of us were praying for them. Yet this did not stop us from later praying for another next-door neighbor who almost died after having a rather routine surgery. After several months, he finally got to come home, regained his strength, and is working again. Even his doctors say,

> "You are a miracle that we will be talking about for years. You must have had a lot of people praying for you."

To that he thankfully admits,

"I did!"

When we have prayed and done everything we can and they still die, we must accept it as God's Will and not feel guilty. We have done what the Bible told us to do.

On the other hand, I believe that we can shorten our own lives by choosing wrong lifestyles, or even driving carelessly. We must remember that Satan comes to steal, kill and destroy (John 10:10), but I John 3:8 tells us, "I (Jesus) have come to destroy the works of the devil," and we know that sickness and disease are the works of the devil. That is why Jesus went around healing the sick. Yet, we're told in Matthew 13:58 that Jesus couldn't do many miracles in his hometown because of the unbelief of the people. They must have thought, 'Oh, he's just a carpenter's son.' Are you not getting your healing when someone prays for you because you think that God heals only through prominent pastors and famous evangelists? When someone prays for you in faith, just reach out in your own faith to receive your healing. The object of this book is to encourage ordinary Christians to reach out to God in faith for their needs, and to also pray for the needs of others. You do not need to call for any special person to pray for you. God is no respecter of persons. Pray for yourselves and each other in faith, but <u>always</u> pray in the Name of Jesus.

We have told you just a few of the many answers to prayer that we have had, but our lives have not been without trials. We have both lost our parents, and Gertrude has lost eight of her siblings. From another standpoint, being in business was not easy, especially in the early years. When our family was giving programs, our 18-year-old guitar player (Don) was killed in an automobile accident. Dawn and Penny were just in their teens when that happened, yet Don had become so close to us that he was 'the son we never had.' He was so excited when he found out that we were going to cut an album in Nashville that he woke his parents to tell them the news. Since he never got to play with us on that album because of his death, we dedicated the album to Don. Later, his youngest brother played for us, but when Penny married, her husband took over the guitar playing duties.

After about four years of marriage, our first daughter, Dawn, was born in 1950. Her sister, Penny, was born three years later in 1953, yet we raised them both while running our restaurant. Our "tag along,"

Candy, was born in 1962. By then we had bought adjoining land to manufacture our *Hit Archery* bows, and, later, trophies. We discontinued the restaurant and converted the building into our archery and trophy showroom.

> *[Gertrude has always been there for our children and grandchildren so, as she writes the rest of this, it will be her words because their health and problems are etched deeply into her heart and mind.]*

Dawn seemed to be the one to get all the childhood diseases more seriously than the other two. Early in her marriage when she was very ill, I, Gertrude, took her to the doctor. When he examined her and saw the unusual curvature of her spine, he asked Dawn when she had polio? Dawn just looked at me with astonishment. I answered,

> *"We didn't know that she did, but when she was a child she was very ill for an entire week with a fever." Nowadays they would put a child that sick in the hospital. [I can remember asking the doctor at that earlier time, with tears running down my cheeks, "Can't you do something?"]*

He gave her some medicine from which she later broke out in a rash. We thought it was the measles, even though she had had that childhood illness. (Oh, if I had only known at that time that we could take authority over the fever and sickness in the name of Jesus. The Bible says, "My people perish for lack of knowledge," but our church did not teach that.)

As the girls got older, when we traveled to archery tournaments around the area we always took them along with us. We sang and harmonized together in the car as we traveled. When we went to the migrant camps to minister, we also took them along and sang, which was the start of our singing together as *The Gospel Hits*. About the time we began giving programs, Dawn was becoming frail and used to frequently get flue-like symptoms. Sometimes she could barely talk, but she would still go in faith and sing with us. If she felt so bad that she couldn't go, Candy would take her place, as even in her teens Candy had such a range of voice that she could sing most any vocal part. Two weeks before Dawn and Tom were to be married, Dawn became so ill that we thought we might have to postpone the wedding; however, we did not. This condition went on, but thankfully she was able to use her beautiful voice when we recorded two albums in Nashville. After Tom and Dawn were married two years, she sought further medical help. Lupus was not heard of much at that time, but it was the disease that she was finally diagnosed as having (Systemic Lupus Erathematosis), a disease of the immune system that attacks the body's vital organs. Wherever we sang, we requested prayer for her. To add to their woes, Dawn's first child was stillborn. We had our own private funeral and buried little Frankie James.

After much prayer and medication, the Lupus went into remission but the damage had already been done to her system. Bud said to Tom,

"Dawn may not be strong enough to have children, so you may have to adopt."

Tom replied,

"I've thought of that."

I got a little angry at all that and said,

"She will have a healthy child! Pray!"

Well, Dawn did get pregnant and our miracle grandson, Abraham Joseph, was born. He was so cute that everyone thought that he was a girl until Tom said,

"Get that boy's hair cut!"

I must say that he is all boy because by the time he was two years old he was watching sports on TV. He still watches sports and has been an active participant in various sports throughout his school years. Those were very happy years.

In spite of Dawn's struggle with health, she would have good times along with the bad. In the meantime, Penny had married and given us our first beautiful curly-haired granddaughter, Kami. Three years later, Dan was born, and six years later Krista came into this world. I baby-sat a lot for my precious grandchildren and, one time, when Abe was about nine years old and Penny's Krista was about two, I had them both at my house. They were having so much fun that I said to Abe,

"Wouldn't you like to have a baby sister?"

He said,

"Yes, but I don't want Mama to get sick again."

I replied,

"We will ask Jesus to give you a baby sister and that Mama will be healthier than ever."

So we knelt down together and prayed for that to happen. We didn't tell Dawn and Tom but, you guessed it, a couple of months later Dawn called and said that she was pregnant. That was honestly as much of a shock to both of them as it was to the doctors, as they didn't think that after all the medication she had taken she would even be able to get pregnant again.

One day about a month later I was reading my Bible while also listening to it on the cassette recorder. I generally read through the Bible every year, but I had never before listened to the Scripture on tape at the same time I was reading it. Just then the phone rang and it was Dawn, so I just pushed the stop button on the recorder. She was upset and told me that the doctor's office had called and asked her to go to the hospital immediately because what she thought was a baby may be nothing more than a tumor. What a heartbreak those words were! However, that was their preliminary diagnosis due to one of Dawn's blood test numbers being higher than normal. So I prayed with her on the phone and then called Bud, who was at work at the time, and some of our Christian friends to pray for her. I prayed and had a peace about things, and then decided to go back to my reading and listening to the Bible on tape. When I hit the play button to resume the recording, the next words were, " **And none will miscarry or be barren in the land, and I will give you a full life span." At that, I hit the stop button and just began praising the Lord! There has always been some Scripture to come along just when I needed it most.** I have held onto the words, **"a full life span,"** whenever Dawn has her bad times. Several hours later, Dawn called me back and said,

"It's a baby!"

I told her what had happened and she said,

"Oh, that's neat."

On our 41st wedding anniversary, Dawn had a C-section and, while Tom was with her in the delivery room, we were in the waiting room and 10-year-old Abe was running around the hospital grounds excitedly awaiting the arrival of his sibling. The nurse came down and said that Dawn was fine and that we had a <u>healthy</u> grandchild, but that Tom wanted the privilege of telling us what gender it was. As we proceeded to the elevator with the nurse, I said to Abe,

> "They don't have to tell us what gender it is because we already know that it's a girl since we asked Jesus for a baby sister for you."

We could tell by the surprised look on the nurse's face that it in fact was a girl. Tiffany became, and still is, Daddy's little girl. We tease her and tell her how much he spoils her. Along with the Lupus, Dawn had contracted Raynaud's disease, which limits the use of her hands, so much so that Tiffany became mama's little helper. Big brother Abe taught Tiffany to play basketball, so she was on the school team. Of course, Dawn, Tom, and Abe never missed any of her games. As of this writing, Tiffany is 19 and attending a college close to home.

Dawn's health has been about the same for the last several years, though with no emergencies, for which we are thankful, considering that she does have leakage of the heart and other physical problems. A number of years ago, they tried to stretch Dawn's mitral valve, which was not successful, and they actually "lost her" on the operating table but were able to revive her. Another time the doctor had her rushed to Ann Arbor hospital via ambulance where they have disease specialists. She has lost her hair in various experimental treatments, but it has always grown back.

Yet there is much for which we are thankful. Dawn can still care for herself and seldom misses church. She is always ready to go places when someone asks and I still drive her to most of her appointments. She has a housecleaner that comes in weekly, but Dawn still insists on doing her own laundry. The last few years she has received a small disability check. After she sets aside her tithe, she can use the balance for personal necessities that she cannot do for herself, such as a manicure, pedicure, haircut, etc. Once a month she has lunch with a couple of girls with whom she graduated. This all gives her a feeling of independence and self-sufficiency. I thank God for those two girls because it gives Dawn something to look forward to. When we wintered in the south, Dawn often flew down to spend several weeks with us, so we definitely praise God for the years we have had her. We knew of a girl who was Dawn's age who was diagnosed with the same disease at about the same time Dawn was, but she lived to be only 29. By God's grace and continued prayers, Dawn just turned 56. We are thankful for her faithful, hardworking husband who, after a day at work, has to come home and do things that Dawn cannot do on her own, and we certainly praise God for the two grandchildren they have given us. She may not have gotten the complete healing that we asked God for, but we haven't given up praying. [I am as persistent as the widow in Luke 18:1-8.]

To add to Dawn and Tom's trials, in 1994 Tom was taking his family out for lunch after church when a lady went around another car on a curve and hit their van head-on. Abe took off his new shirt and wrapped it around his unconscious dad's head that was bleeding profusely, and then left little Tiffy and Dawn, who were both bruised and crying, to run for help. After calling 9-1-1, he called us saying that his dad was in a bad way and to please hurry. Though we were breaking the speed limit all the way to the crash site, I was begging God to save Tom's life. I will never forget the scene of four ambulances and police cars with flashing lights. As we tried to make our way through the crowd that had gathered, we kept saying,

"That's our family—let us through!"

We found, Dawn, Tiffany, and Abe already on stretchers while other paramedics were trying desperately to get Tom's unconscious body out of the van. Finally they did, and with sirens screaming I rode in the ambulance with them to the Bryan hospital, praying all the way. It was scary when I heard them giving Tom's vitals via their voice-radio system. Life Flight arrived and immediately transferred Tom to Toledo. I checked the rest of them into the hospital and then called Tom's parents and my other girls. At that time, Tiffany was crying so much for me to come. Dawn said she herself was bruised only slightly and that I should just go to Tiffany. When I got to her room, her little arm was badly sprained but, after praying and trying to comfort her, I left her with Penny who had arrived with her family. They discharged the three of them that same day, so Penny stayed with them all night while Tom's brother took Tom's mother and me to Toledo for Tom's operation. His leg had to be rodded, but his heel was crushed so badly that the surgeon said he had nothing to go by and that he could only put it back together the way he thought would be best, given its crushed condition. It was good that Tom was so physically strong because his recovery took all the strength he had. I moved in with them for about two months to care for the family.

Later, Tom's mother relieved me at nights so that I could get a good night's sleep. Because Candy and Alan lived in Connecticut at the time, she asked for a leave from her job and flew home the following day for a week. As soon as Tom was discharged from the hospital, the therapists came and he started managing the business via the phone, and later from a recliner that they took to the shop. Of course Bud went back to the shop to help as long as he was needed. Though Tom doesn't complain, he still suffers with pain in that heel but it hasn't slowed him down. I am glad that many of the good workers we had when we owned the business continued working there, and Abe has joined his father in the business.

In spite of all Dawn and Tom's physical problems and trials, God provided another miracle in 1999. Their son, Abe, was on his motorcycle heading for the shop to have lunch with his Dad when the driver of a pickup truck did not see him coming and turned right in front of him, hitting him head on. It was so hot that August day that Abe was not wearing his helmet, which was (is) not a good idea. Upon impact, he went flying through the air and ended up in a large blue spruce tree, which cushion likely saved his life. Yet God intervened and, even without the helmet, Abe had no head injuries or any marks on his handsome face. Though he had a whole list of other serious injuries, he never lost consciousness and through all the injuries and pain, he said,

"I'm still going to play basketball, grandpa!"

They life-flighted Abe to a Toledo hospital where they found that he had both legs broken, both kidneys punctured, both lungs punctured, his liver lacerated, his back compressed, both arms broken, and a bone missing from one of the arms. He was critical that first week, but was able to go through three restorative operations. This happened on a Monday and the following Friday after another operation he was in so much pain that even the morphine couldn't take it away. He became so discouraged that he told his Dad,

"Take me home; they aren't telling me anything."

We knew that was impossible, so I stayed by his bedside all night praying and taking care of his needs. They had hung his arms up in angel slings, which he begged to have taken down, but the nurses would not. When he begged me to do it for him, I knew that I dared not. It just broke my heart when at 2:00 A.M. that morning he asked me,

"Gram, how long was Jesus on the cross?"

[He probably was lying there in his pain thinking how long Jesus had hung on the cross with His arms raised.]

Our assistant pastor, Louie, had come that night. He is so compassionate; I can still remember the breaks in his voice as he prayed for Abe. Many were praying for this athletic young Christian who had just gotten his referee's license. Tiffany never missed a day of going to see her big brother.

Since Abe had been active in sports, was president of his high school class, was active with the young adults at church, and has personality plus, he had tons of company—so much so that they decided to give him a private room! I think the nurses also fell in love with this young man. Abe was in the hospital for only fifteen days and came home in a wheel chair with a lot of metal in him and on him. He still has a metal bar in his arm, a rod in his leg, surgical screws in his wrists and feet, but even all that isn't enough to deter him from playing basketball. To add to this miracle, the doctors thought that Abe would be shorter due to the compression of his spine but, when he was able to stand and get rid of the turtle shell he wore, he was an inch taller than he had been before the accident! God again showed that He was indeed in control. This happened in 1999, and six months later he scored sixteen points in a church league basketball game. He continues to play basketball and referee. In 2004 he purchased a house and had a living room full of workout equipment until he married in 2005, at which time the equipment was moved! We will never be able to thank God enough for Abe's miracle.

We have four beautiful granddaughters, two handsome grandsons, and four precious great-grandchildren. How the years have flown, and how we have been blessed. You parents and grandparents know that when your children, grandchildren, and great-grandchildren hurt, you hurt.

Abe & wife Angela.

Chapter 32
"Classmates"

During my teenage years, a group of us guys ran around together, my best friend Wes being one of them. Though I was the only one of the group who didn't go to church or Sunday School, when we were all together their actions seemed to be no different than mine. In those days, I suppose we were considered to be a bit wild, but in comparison to what goes on today it was mild. After Wes and I got married, we drifted apart for a while, though it was completely unintentional. We had gone into business for ourselves, and all the work that was demanded kept us so busy that there really wasn't much time to socialize. Years later when Wes rededicated his life to the Lord, it so happened that we both became Gideon's and started attending the Saturday morning jail ministry.

In 1980, Wes and I learned that one of our Christian classmates had to cancel her trip to the Holy Land because of lymphoma cancer. After the jail ministry one Saturday, we decided that we would stop by her house to pray for her. We knocked at the back door and she came out on the porch to see us. She was very happy to know that we had come to pray for her, so we had a brief time of prayer. As God already knows our needs before we ask, a long prayer doesn't necessarily get any better results than a short-and-to-the-point-prayer. Later we heard that she did indeed go on the trip and that the cancer had become dormant. Some call it "remission," but I call it "healing" by the power of Almighty God. She is still very active and goes to Florida every winter.

A few years later we had a class reunion where each member was asked to give a short review of their life and what had taken place with them since the last reunion. When it came to her turn, she said,

"I probably have more to be thankful for than anyone here."

She then told them all about her bout with cancer starting in 1979 and how her condition had turned for the worse in 1980, so much so that she was going to cancel her planned trip to the Holy Land. Then she related how God had touched her and that she did go on the trip. She added,

"Two of the most unlikely fellow classmates came to my home and prayed for me, and I haven't had the cancer problem since!"

Unlikely yes, the way we were in school I guess, but God forgave our sins and washed them clean in the Blood of Jesus Christ. After we both decided to give every part of our lives to God, He was able to use us for His honor and glory. What a privilege it is to serve a loving, forgiving God who still does miracles when we pray in faith using the Name of Jesus. John 14:13-14 and Colossians 3:17 tell us that everything we say or do, we should do in the Name of Jesus.

Chapter 33
"My Aching Back"

One day I called for a tee-time at our golf course at Sun City, Hilton Head, where we wintered for six years. I had not been able to play much because of some back pain that I had been experiencing. I certainly wasn't able to hit the short clubs because I couldn't bend over far enough. When I arrived at the clubhouse that day, they put me with a man and his wife. As the three of us were waiting for others that were ahead of us to play some of the holes, I began sharing with them some of the miracles I had seen God perform. I could tell that wasn't something they were accustomed to hearing, but they politely listened and then told me where they went to church. I suspected that what I was telling them was not practiced in their church.

We were on the fairway of the fifth hole and I was getting ready to hit my second shot when the back pain hit me so hard that I couldn't even swing my club. In fact, I could barely stoop down to pick up my ball. I walked over to the cart where the lady sat alone, as her husband was some distance away hitting his ball. I told her that I was sorry, but I could not continue because the pain was too bad, so I was going home. She quietly said that she wanted to pray for me and proceeded to do so. It was a simple prayer that went something like this.

"Jesus, take away the pain and heal Bud so he can play golf."

I was sure she had never done that before, but, praise the Lord, I straightened right up and, with no pain, finished the game—and that was the end of my extreme pain! I had sold my short irons due to the pain in bending over. Since I buy the heads and make my own clubs, I made a new set of short irons. Gertrude did not know whom the lady was that prayed for me, but later she played with that same lady in the ladies' league. When the lady found out that Gertrude was my wife, she asked her how my back was. Still not knowing the lady, Gertrude just replied that a lady had prayed for him and he had no more pain. When Gertrude later saw her name on the scorecard, she remarked,

"You're the one who prayed for him! Thank you so much!"

This is another example why we are to tell others what God has done, as it encourages them to step out in faith and pray for others.

Chapter 34
"Only Half a Kidney"

While wintering in South Carolina, Bill & Marty, our dear friends who were responsible for us moving from Florida to Sun City, South Carolina, started a Bible study in their home. A pastor and his wife led the Bible study, and one evening they brought a young couple along with them. The young wife was about seven months into her pregnancy and had been informed by the doctors that her unborn baby boy might not live outside the womb. They said that what should be his kidney was only a growth and not a kidney at all, and that the second kidney was only half the size it should be, making it next to impossible for the baby to live once it was born. When it was time for prayer, the ladies gathered around the young mother-to-be, laid hands on her, and prayed in the Name of Jesus for God to give the baby two complete kidneys.

About two months later, I received a call at our Ohio home from the pastor's wife telling us that the baby had been born. She said that when the baby came out into the doctor's hands, it "wee-weed" on the doctor. (God has a sense of humor, doesn't He?) When they checked, they found that the baby indeed had two perfect kidneys. Later we were told that the doctors were trying to get the young mother to see a specialist in Charleston so that they could find out what actually happened. Sometimes it is difficult for people to believe that our God still performs miracles!

Chapter 35
"Just One More Bite!"

In 2001 one of Gertrude's sisters was in a rehabilitation center after having had another stroke. We went to visit her around lunchtime in the cafeteria, and then sat with her while she ate. I noticed that at one of the tables was a nurse who was trying to feed a certain man. She would say to him,

"Please just take one bite."

His wife was also trying to encourage him to eat. Later we found out that, after his stroke, the man could eat only a small bite now and then, so they had taken him to the Bryan Hospital and put in a stomach feeding tube. They returned him to rehab to do everything that they could to get him to eat. After lunch, we pushed sister Polly back to her room and, since other relatives had come to visit, I decided to see whom else I could visit. [I might add here that I have found that people in rehab are always glad for visitors.] I peeked into the next room and there was the man who had not been able to eat for weeks, his wife sitting by his bedside. I introduced myself and started chatting about different things, and then asked if I could pray for him. They both agreed, instantly saying that they, too, believed in prayer. I just had a short and simple prayer asking God to restore his desire and ability to eat. I always ask in the Name of Jesus, just as the Bible says we should. As I have said before, God knows our needs even before we ask, but He nevertheless wants us to ask—in faith—so I always try to get "right to the point" with a short prayer. After praying, I left the room and went to another room where a lady was sitting at the bedside of a woman, who I later learned was her mother. To my surprise she said,

"Aren't you Bud Hitt?"

I replied that I was. [They explained that they had seen me in the cafeteria and knew me from living in the area.] The mother, who had lost her ability to speak due to a stroke, wrote my name on a piece of paper saying that she had met me years ago and that she was a friend of my sister. I visited for a while and then asked if I could pray for her speech to be restored. She nodded her head, so again I prayed a very short prayer asking God to restore her speech and then we left. When we returned in a couple of days to see Polly, I of course wanted to visit the people that I had prayed for a few days earlier. When I walked into the room of the man who had not been able to eat for several weeks, I was greeted by his wife who excitedly told me that the same day we prayed for her husband's appetite to return, it did, and that she now was bringing some of his favorite foods from home for him to eat in-between meals. Isn't God good! When I crossed the hall to go to the room of the lady who had not been able to speak, she greeted me herself! Her speech had returned and she said that her daughter was taking her home that same day! Praise the Lord! He's not only our Savior, but our Healer as well.

However, as much as we prayed for Gertrude's sister, Polly, she had several more strokes and soon was moved to a more intensive-care facility in Toledo. One time, on the way home from a niece's wedding in Pennsylvania, we stopped by to visit her. The last stroke had left her very weak and had also taken her speech. The nurse said that if she got stronger, they would try speech therapy. Prior to her being moved to Toledo, Gertrude would visit her at the local Rest Home and sing as many as twenty hymns to Polly, who would do her best to sing along on every verse. On this visit, Gertrude said to her,

"Polly, remember how we sang together when you were at the nursing home? Let's try to sing like that again."

As Gertrude started to sing, to everyone's amazement, including our own, Polly joined her in singing, though very weakly. The nurse who was passing by the door, stopped and looked in with utter surprise, not believing what she was hearing. Polly still could not talk, but on that day she could sing! This is an example of the principle that what we put into our hearts and minds is what will come out, particularly when the going gets tough. If we put complaining and cursing in, that's what comes out. If we put Scripture and praise songs in, then that's what comes out. Polly had songs in her heart and mind, as well as Scripture that we recited together at the first Rest Home when she could still talk. The Word was in her and so that's what came out in her time of testing!

Although many family, friends, and pastors prayed for her, God took Polly home to be with Him shortly after that visit. As I've said before, we should always ask in faith believing, and then let the results up to God. We still miss Polly, but know that she is not struggling anymore and is now happy beyond words, having joined her husband and young son in Heaven.

As I, Gertrude, am typing this manuscript for Bud, the above story brings to my remembrance an incident that happened to me a number of years ago. I visited a lady at our local Rest Home who was in a wheelchair, and, as we talked that day, I simply knelt down at her wheelchair and said a simple prayer for her. Though I didn't know her personally at the time, I learned that she was the mother of a friend of mine who lived in the next woods over from our place. My friend later told me that she will never forget the first time she saw me—I was on my knees in front of her mother's wheelchair at the Rest Home, rubbing her swollen legs and praying for her. She proceeded to tell me that her mother had been a minister and that she could not carry on a conversation or remember much of anything, but that she could still preach. She had hidden God's Word in her heart and it did not return void.

Chapter 36
"Who Opened the Door?"

In 2001 when we still wintered in South Carolina, we saw one of the most unusual workings of God that Gertrude and I have ever seen. We flew home for the Holidays one winter to spend a beautiful Christmas with our family. The summer before, at one of our family reunions, we sat with Gertrude's cousin Mary and her husband, both of them our ages. That was the first we knew Mary was having a bout with cancer, so we had a short prayer right there at the table with them. Now, back to our Christmas Holiday with the family... It was New Year's Eve day and, with our return flight to South Carolina being less than 48 hours away, Gertrude called Mary and asked if we could come over and see her before we left. She said,

"Yes, please do. I want you to."

When we arrived at her house about 6:00 P.M., her daughter was there with Mary and her husband, though she was just ready to leave. I asked Mary if she could go to a restaurant for a little while with us. Mary immediately agreed, but her daughter wasn't sure that her mother should go because it was so cold outside. However, as Mary insisted that she would be fine, the daughter agreed and left for home and then the four of us went to a little restaurant. After eating, we returned to the mobile home park in which they lived and drove up under the car canopy about 15 feet from their front door where they had left the outside light on. It was only about nine degrees (F) when we got out of the car. When Skip, Mary's husband, reached into his pocket for the key to unlock the door, he realized that all of his keys were in their car which he had taken to the garage that afternoon. He said,

"Mary, where are your keys?"

Mary replied,

"In my purse in the house."

Gertrude and I both tried to open the door, but it was locked tight so we quickly got Mary back into our car and started questioning her as to who was the nearest neighbor that might have a spare key, but there was no one. (It is a good idea to leave a key with a trusted neighbor like we do.) Gertrude offered to take them to our house, but Mary said that her medication was in the house.

The problem got bigger when Skip said that he didn't know the owner's name or any of the mechanics down at the garage. As the three of us sat in our car, Skip went about 30 feet to his little tool shed and returned with a big claw hammer. Mary yelled out the window and asked him to please not break their pretty window in the door. I quickly said,

"Let's ask the Lord to open the door somehow."

Very briefly I said something like this,

"God, you know that we are in a mess and do not know what to do, so we ask in the Name of Jesus that you open that door for us. I don't know how you are going to do it, but we know that you can. Thank you, Lord."

Skip decided to take the claw part of the hammer and put it under the lip of the door to pry it open. As the three of us watched him reach for the door, it slowly opened! Skip was so startled that he jumped back with the hammer raised in his hand saying,

"I didn't even touch the door!"

We began thanking and praising the Lord for what we had just witnessed and quickly got Mary into her warm home. Sitting inside the house, we couldn't help but marvel and praise the Lord for this miracle. Mary had not been able to go to Sunday School for awhile, but said that she just had to go the following Sunday and share this miracle. It was time for us to leave for the night, but we kept in contact with them via phone and e-mail from our winter home. She said that she did go to Sunday School and told them what had happened.

Although many of us prayed for Mary, a few days after we returned to Ohio for the summer, Mary went to be with her Lord. Mary's memorial service was one of the best we have ever been to. Her son, who is a video specialist, took individual photos that she had accumulated from childhood, their courtship, and the early and later days of their marriage, and integrated them into an amazing video that we all viewed from a large screen in the church. Mary was a classy lady and never allowed her illness to detract from her physical appearance. She even had her nails done shortly before her death. After the memorial service, Skip told Gertrude and me that the opening of the door was a highlight for Mary and really boosted her faith. He said that it was a way for God to show Mary that He really loved her and that He was so concerned for her in those moments that He provided a miracle for her to get back into her warm home. I might say that it boosted our faith also! We give God all the glory for answering our prayer, as we felt desperate at the time.

I do not know why all of our prayers aren't answered. Perhaps if they were, people might look to us instead of to God, Who, in His mercy, is the One who really does it. He only desires that we ask in faith.

Chapter 37
"Goodbye Sun City"

After six years of wintering at Sun City, South Carolina, it became almost too much to keep up two homes. We paid someone to do the yard in S. C. while we were in Ohio for the summer, but they only mowed and didn't do any other yard work. So when we returned for the winter months, there was always a lot to do. Even though it was a new house, the tropic-like climate presented us with many things that needed attention outside. I had told Gertrude the previous year that I thought we should sell it, but she wasn't enthused about that, and for good reasons. She had many friends, golfing and otherwise, and she loved her weekly community Bible Study, as well as all our friends at the Baptist Church we attended, not to mention the milder-than-Ohio winter weather. When I persisted, she said,

> *"Let's pray about it and, if we are to sell, God will send us a buyer before we go home for the summer so that we won't have to think about the yard or any outside maintenance while we're gone."*

So that's what we did. She said that she would call Evelyn, a resident of our community who was also a Realtor, and find out some things about the real estate market and what would be involved. Evelyn came over later and had us fill out some papers. After she left, Gertrude said,

> "I thought that we were just going to get some information and not sign papers to list it right away."

Again we went to prayer. In faith, we put it in the Lord's hands that, if we were to sell, He would bring us the right buyer who would give us the right price, and that it would sell quickly before we left for Ohio. It was difficult for Gertrude to even think about selling the place. Part of her was afraid that if it didn't sell quickly, she might change her mind.

That was in the spring of 2002 when Gertrude was suffering with a left rotator cuff problem, which the Lord has since healed, but at that time my overriding concern was that two places were just too much work. Now I don't mind fixing things and mowing, but I'm not exactly fond of weeding and the other yard work that often needs to be done. The previous winter when we came back down, even though it was a small yard, it took her days to weed the yard. Then when we would return to Ohio each spring, she would start all over again in our large yard and her flower garden. Gertrude was used to working because she was a farm girl (one of ten children) and still spends many hours working out in the yard. [Our middle daughter, Penny, has even more flowers than Gertrude.] One Sunday in church, when the Pastor was talking about heaven, Gertrude slipped me a note that read,

> "Just think—when we get to heaven, I can work in my flowers without having to weed!"

[Gertrude would rather have something that she can plant in the ground than a corsage to wear on Easter or Mother's day. Besides, almost every Mother's Day we were ministering in the jail and corsages are not permitted to be worn because of the pins. As much as we like flowers, when someone dies we give Gideon Memorial Bibles instead so that people can get saved.]

To lay the groundwork for what was about to happen, there were more than 200 houses for resale at Sun City at that time, and our model was the smallest of the different floor plans available. Of those 200+ models, others that were of similar size as ours had been on the market for some time, as many of the people who were selling homes desired larger ones. There were also developments going up all around us with hundreds of new homes for sale. On the plus side, as I am a woodworker and a "jack of all trades," our house had many upgrades and was being sold completely furnished, plus a garage full of tools, which were strong selling points. One day the Realtor brought a single man to look at our house and he seemed to be impressed. Two days later he returned with his daughter to look at it again, but she wanted him to have a larger home.

About a week later, Evelyn brought a couple from New York to look at it, but since they stayed for only 15 to 20 minutes we assumed that they weren't even interested. After they left, we went out to take care of some things that we had on our agenda, and when we returned there was a message on our answering machine from the Realtor saying that the couple had made an offer. Because the couple was staying over for only a few days, Evelyn wanted to come over that evening to explain things to us. She presented us with their offer, knowing that we likely wouldn't accept it, but suggested that we make a counter offer. After the three of us agreed on a fair price, she left to present it to them. In about 15 minutes she called back and said,

> "Congratulations, you have just sold your house! You have set a record for a house being on the market and selling so quickly!"

We knew that it must have been God's Will, which made it easier for Gertrude to accept leaving a place that she loved so much.

I, too, dislike the Ohio winters, so the next year we rented an apartment at a mobile home court for January and February in Bradenton, Florida. Our Ohio home is in a quiet neighborhood in the country, so we were not accustomed to all the night sirens from the nearby fire and police stations, and thus declined the offer to go back there. We called our dear friend in Florida, Hixon, who was my golfing buddy and neighbor when we wintered at *Christian Retreat* near Bradenton, and asked him if he could find us a place to rent on the grounds there. We had just about given up hope, but I said to Gertrude,

> "Let's just stay here in Ohio for the winter. We have this new well-insulated garage that I can quickly heat up to work in, and also my workshop in the basement. Besides, if we remain here for the winter, we won't need to have someone take our place at the jail."

She agreed, but just said a short prayer,

"Lord, if you want us to have a place to rent at Christian Retreat, find us something <u>unexpected</u>."

Note the word <u>unexpected</u>, because in less than 20 minutes the phone rang and it was our friend Hixon. He said that the duplex, two houses down from where we previously had wintered for nine years, was empty except for a few weeks every year. The couple that owned it was from New York, but because they were not yet retired, they came down only a few weeks each winter. Since Hixon was on the board, he was able to give us their phone number, but when Gertrude called the lady, she very emphatically said that they would not rent it because of some bad rental experiences. Gertrude told her to contact any of the three pastors and that they would vouch for us. Since we had both put in many hours of volunteer work and taught in the school of Ministry, we were well known to the staff. Gertrude assured her that nothing would be taken and that we would leave it clean. When the lady still said "No," I whispered in my wife's ear,

"Tell her that we attend a Mennonite church in Ohio."

When she did the lady said,

"That's the best thing you've said yet. I am in my prayer time right now, but I will talk to my husband and call you back."

(Mennonites have a reputation for being clean, honest, thrifty, dependable, hard working, and always being there to help those in need, though I admit there are exceptions to the rule.)

In about 20 minutes her husband phoned and said that we could have it. I told him that I was handy in fixing things and would take care of it as if it were my own. When he replied that he couldn't fix anything, when we left for Florida I took my toolbox along. Because the couple hadn't been there much, the place was in need of some tender love and care, which I was able to give it. After spending the winter there, buying them a new washing machine and doing some needed repairs, they invited us to come back the following winter. We liked staying there at *Christian Retreat* because it was like "being home," seeing old friends and meeting new ones. To us, once you visit *Christian Retreat*, you have to go back. There are duplexes, condos, two hotels, a mobile home park, cafeteria, campground, school of ministry, and conference center where well-known speakers from all over the world come. Co-pastors Gerald and Phil Derstine are two of the best Bible teachers you will ever hear.

About three weeks before leaving for Florida the following winter, I acquired a severe toothache. I went to a local dentist who, after x-raying and checking me out, said that he didn't pull teeth anymore. I had to wonder why he didn't tell me that when I phoned and told him that I needed a tooth pulled—it would have saved me some money! He gave me a phone number to call a professional of his who would take care of what I needed to have done. However, when I phoned that man I was told they were in the process of moving to a new location and weren't able to help me until the following week. In the meantime, Gertrude had found a numbing liquid that I could put on my tooth that took away the immediate pain. As the days went by, and with the effectiveness of the numbing liquid, I got so busy making final preparations to go to Florida that I neglected to call the dentist back. When departure day came, off to Florida we went with my tooth being OK for the time being.

However, about three weeks after arriving in Florida I couldn't stop the pain even with the numbing application. Digressing a little for the sake of the story, five mornings a week from 8:30 to 9:30 *Christian Retreat* residents and visitors have a prayer-and-share time in the hotel led by different volunteers. When we owned there previously, we led that prayer-and-share time on Friday mornings and so we went. When it came time for prayer, I asked if they would pray that I find a good dentist who would pull the tooth and that I would have no problems with the procedure. We returned to the house, looked up a dentist in the yellow pages, and called him; however, the receptionist said that they couldn't take me for several weeks. Instead, she gave me the number of another dentist who was located near where we were staying. It was 10:00 A.M. when we called and, to my surprise, they said that I should be there by noon. I asked if they could pull the tooth that day and they said they could because they had an oral surgeon on staff.

When I got there and walked into the room I thought, "This man is as old as I am!"

He looked my situation over and, as I talked about the Lord, I discovered that he was a brother in Christ. He had to take out my tooth piece by piece because the root was so intertwined with my jawbone. As it turned out, he was one of the best oral surgeons I could have found. He gave me a prescription for pain pills, which I ended up not even needing.

During that week our oldest daughter, Dawn, flew down to Bradenton and so the three of us went back to have my stitches taken out. When he finished removing them, he said,

"I have something to tell you that I can't tell just anyone, but I know you will understand."

He told me that he lived in St. Petersburg, which is across the Skyway Bridge from Bradenton, and that he had to pass the airport every morning to go to work. The traffic was always so heavy that it was next to impossible for him to get through morning rush hour, as he had to turn left through the traffic at several busy intersections. Since it was so nerve wracking to him, he said that he asked the Lord to allow him to get through the traffic that morning without any problems. He then said that when he came to the airport intersections that morning, there wasn't one car in either lane, something he had never experienced before!

We praised the Lord together and I left without any problems whatsoever from what had been rather extensive oral surgery. Besides his professional skill, what made the extra difference for me was knowing that I was in the hands of a brother in Christ.

Chapter 38
"Only a Little Scar"

I never had any brothers, but I do have a sister who is 2½ years older than I, and another younger sister, Diana, who is 13 years younger. Since Diana had worn glasses for most of her life, she went to see the optometrist one day for a routine eye exam. After the doctor examined her eyes, he gave her a rather devastating prognosis—she had macular degeneration and glaucoma. He told her there was nothing that could be done for her. Totally in shock when she returned home, she phoned her four daughters, three of whom still lived in the Archbold area, who came over to try to comfort their mother. After the initial shock, Dana, her youngest, went to her computer to do some research about the two diseases. After she found out how debilitating they can be, she declared to the family,

"I am <u>not</u> going to receive this diagnosis for mom!"

She called her Christian friends to pray for her Mother's healing, and also put it on an e-mail prayer chain. She then made an appointment for her mother to see a specialist at the *Kellogg Eye Center* in Ann Arbor, Michigan. The day for the appointment arrived and, after a very thorough examination, they anxiously awaited the specialist's results. To their absolute joy, he had good news. He said that the only thing he could find was a little scar on her retina, about an eighth of an inch long, and that otherwise her eyes were fine! The only conclusion we could draw was that God had left a little scar to show her (and us) that something <u>had</u> been wrong but that He had made it whole. The Bible says in James 4:2, "You have not, because you ask not." Jesus said in John 14:12, "Anyone who has faith in me will do the works I have been doing."

As of this writing, it has been about five years since God healed my sister's eyes. As an addendum to this story, Diana took a series of lessons in "One-stroke Painting" and has become so good at it that the instructor told her she couldn't teach Diana anything more. It takes good eyes to put out the beautiful professional work that Diana does. Thank God for a daughter who believes that God answers prayer!

Chapter 39
"Spurs, Be Gone!"

When we still wintered at Sun City Hilton Head, South Carolina, Gertrude started having pain in her heel that was subsequently diagnosed as bone spurs, which are jagged buildups of calcium that jab the flesh when pressure is put on them. She was given special padded shoes that gave her some relief. Since it was spring and we would soon be heading back to our home in Ohio, she decided to wait and see a podiatrist there. After we arrived home, a podiatrist took x-rays, verified that it was spurs, gave her a cortisone shot in the heel, and then made an appointment for her to return. When there still was no relief, we returned and he gave her another cortisone shot. The doctor said that if that didn't work she would have to have an operation.

Shortly after being back, it was our time to do the Sunday morning services at the Five-County correctional jail. The halls are very long that lead back to the classroom where the services are held. With much pain and my help, Gertrude was able to get down the long hallways. The requirement is that there must be at least two volunteer chaplains present and, since the inmates like to sing, Gertrude always opens the service by leading them in some praise songs on her Omnichord. After she had finished playing and had the opening prayer, she said to the ladies,

"I have prayed for you many times, but now it's your turn to pray for me."

She related to them about the foot problem she was having and the fact that she did not want to have the operation. I asked the ladies who believed that they had faith for her healing to lay hands on her and agree in prayer for her healing. A group of them gathered around my wife and one lady bent over, laid her hands on Gertrude's foot and said,

"You go in the name of Jesus!"

This she repeated several times, each time a little louder.

Most of the other girls also were agreeing in prayer for Gertrude to be healed. After we had finished the services, we packed up her instrument, picked up our Bibles and started down the long hallways. Gertrude noticed that she could walk much better and that I didn't need to help her. As she walked, she just continued to claim her healing by faith. By the next morning it was better yet, and by the third day all the pain was gone from her foot! This was a "mountain" in Gertrude's life to which the inmate had spoken for it to be removed. Of course, we had prayed many times for her foot, but perhaps the ladies there needed to see that they, too, could pray for others and see God work. They, too, are just ordinary people through whom God wants to work.

It is indeed rewarding to see inmates grow in their faith.

Chapter 40
"Gertrude's Healings"

I (Gertrude) am going to tell you about three dramatic healings that I had, one in 2002 and two in 2004.

I think we might be very surprised about the many times the Lord has kept us from harm or healed us of something that we did not know we had. I have felt his touch many times, yet I know there were many times when I didn't even realize His intervention. If we are healed after six months of suffering, then we know that the Lord has touched us and it is something we will never forget. I never will.

While wintering in South Carolina in December of 2001, I started having pain in my left arm, shoulder, and back that fluctuated from an ache to literal numbness, and eventually to a feeling of heaviness. By February of 2002, the pain was so intense that I had to quit golfing and doing my weight exercises. I had an EKG, blood tests, stress test, shoulder and back x-rays, bone scan, and a bone density test. As a result, I was put on Fosamax for my bones, Cellebrex for the pain, and when that didn't work they prescribed 12.5 mg. of Vioxx that was soon doubled in dosage. I was not accustomed to taking that much medication and it made me depressed. Because we had sold our winter home (prior story), and since I couldn't sleep very well because of the pain, I just stayed up and did all the packing. When we got home to Ohio, I immediately made an appointment with our family doctor who put me into therapy until I could get an appointment with an orthopedic surgeon. After two weeks of therapy, the therapist said that he was only hurting me and not really helping me. Little by little I unpacked the rest of the boxes and slept a little, but then only from sheer exhaustion. Finally, near the end of June 2002, I was able to get in to see the orthopedic surgeon and he confirmed what my family doctor had suspected; it was my rotator cuff. He gave me a cortisone shot that sent me into orbit. My husband told the doctor that in all the years we had been married he never heard me scream. The doctor said that he must have hit the rotator cuff or the bone. After the initial pain, I was free of pain, but four hours later I couldn't lift my arm or use my fingers. However, after that brief time of freedom, the pain became even worse than before. Finally, I called the surgeon who then doubled my Vioxx to 50 mg. While that dosage, along with continuous ice packs, helped some, the higher dosage made me even more depressed, so I tried to keep busy to take my mind off the pain. After we did the jail services the following Sunday, I told Bud I just couldn't go to church for the second service but felt that I needed to go to bed until it was time to leave for our Care Group meeting at 1:00 P.M. I had made a huge salad and was determined to go since it was the last one of the year, which I did.

After lunch the Care Group leader asked if anyone needed prayer, and of course all us seniors gave our prayer requests. When it came my turn, I said that I just had to have relief from the shoulder pain or I couldn't continue helping Bud at the jail. The leader asked our church's prayer coordinator, David, who was also an elder, to pray for all our needs. [By the way, David is editing and compiling these manuscripts for us.] We never really knew David on a personal level before that day, but he and his wife Judy have since become close friends. I can still see in my mind where I was seated around the table and, as David prayed for the others, I agreed in prayer with him, as I am sure we all did. When he prayed for me, my inner being was silently, but literally, begging for a touch from the Lord **and I received it.** From that time on, I have never taken another Vioxx and I finally slept that night. I can never thank God enough for His merciful touch, and for David who is a real intercessor and prays for many people. He has kept us on his prayer list for which I am thankful, as at our age something in our bodies always needs prayer. I was again able to golf and resume all of my work.

In 2003 I golfed in my ladies' league, as well as with my husband, during what was a very busy summer. Just to give the reader an idea of how much I could do after my healing, Bud and I unloaded lots of sand and black dirt for our lawn that needed reseeded. Using landscaping retaining blocks, Bud made several planters that I filled with shrubs and perennials. I even restored my flower garden that had become trampled during the building of our new garage. That same summer, Bud decided that he was going to put in a 4,000-brick driveway, so, along with my normal housework and daily schedule, I carried bricks for him to mortar into a driveway, though I admit that I was glad when a friend came and relieved me until Bud devised a way of carrying his own. I said, "Why didn't you think of that sooner?"

It was September 2003, and our ladies' golf league was over. My partner (who is a much better golfer than I) and I had taken first place with the low team gross. The golf banquet we had planned was a success; the caterer did a great job. I left the restaurant, put my things into the back seat, and settled into the driver's seat to return home. As I reached over into the back seat for something, a pain suddenly shot up my right shoulder. It wasn't as bad as the left one had been and, with Tylenol PM, I could at least sleep at night, but I could not golf for the next ten months. You may think that golfing is a waste of time, but I feel that everyone needs something besides their work to keep them fresh. You can get so bogged down with others' problems that you burn out.

After we returned from Florida in March of 2004, my local golf partner was wondering if I would be able to play golf that summer due to my shoulder. Since I had been having problems going up and down stairs and walking very far for the last couple of years, on March 19th I went to the orthopedic surgeon who had put an artificial knee in for my 86-year-old sister. After more x-rays, he found that my right knee was bone-on-bone, and that I also had disorders of the bursae and tendons in my right shoulder. He suggested a cortisone shot and so I told him what had happened before when his partner had given me a shot in the left shoulder. I didn't relish the thought of going through that again with my right one, but he promised that he would be careful. It did help some, but I credit prayer more than anything. I alerted David to my problems with the opposite shoulder and right knee and asked him to pray for all my joints. Thanks to answered prayer, I was (and still am) able to golf.

So I decided against a suggested total knee replacement and, instead, made arrangements to have a partial knee resurfacing done in Florida during January of 2005.

My bone problem could be the result of a lack of calcium. I never drank milk as a young girl, as I hated the smell of the cows, which I had to take a half-mile to the woods in the morning for pasture and then go back to get them at night. In the summer, I had to tend the cows as they grazed and ate the grass along the road. I was to make sure they never left that half-mile grazing range or turned the corner toward the neighbors' farms. I remember once, when I was reading, some of them "turned the corner." I was so scared. I kept praying as I ran that I could get them back with the rest of the herd. God answered my prayer and spared me from the whipping I knew I would get. (You have heard that woodsheds were used for more than storing wood, and ours was no exception.)

My Dad took the Bible literally where it tells us that if we spare the rod, we spoil the child. I guess with ten children, of whom I am the youngest girl, and with twin brothers six years younger, I could understand how mom and dad could easily lose their patience. In my younger days, there really wasn't the information as to how important calcium and vitamins were. At least if there was, we were too busy to hear it. Bud and I take a lot of vitamins now and feel blessed that we are able to work as hard as we do and can even get up early to get in some golf. Bud is really a good golfer, though he did not start until he was 64 years old (I started a year later). He can out-drive men much younger than him.

Four days after I had seen the orthopedic doctor, I awoke at 2:00 A.M. with pain below my ribs that I thought was gas. I took antacids, got in and out of bed, and walked the floor. Finally, at 3:00 A.M., I went to the basement and continued with a job I had started the night before. When Bud got up at 5:00 and saw that I was up working, he began scolding me since I had worked late the night before and don't get enough sleep as it is. I explained the situation and, when I still had no relief at 10:00 A.M., he insisted that I call the doctor. My doctor was on vacation but, when I refused to go to the emergency room, the nurse worked me in with another doctor at 2:00 P.M. The blood test showed that I had an acute case of pancreatis and needed to go to the hospital immediately. I protested, but the doctor said if I didn't go, I would die. Bud didn't waste any time getting me there. He called many of our friends to pray, as well as those in South Carolina and Florida. Our pastor came that night and he and Bud agreed for my healing.

They ran more tests and I spent the night in Wauseon hospital. The surgeon came in the following day and said that a stone was blocking my bile duct and I would have to be transferred to Toledo Hospital where they would somehow go down my throat to remove it. He explained that since they did not have the facilities in Wauseon to do it, he had lined up two surgeons in Toledo to remove it the next day, which was a Thursday. Then he said that on Friday he would remove my gall bladder and repair a hernia that I did not even know I had. It was depressing to go from our much newer hospital in Wauseon, with its quiet private rooms, to one in Toledo with a roommate who coughed all night. It was impossible to get any sleep in that environment, let alone them checking my vitals and drawing blood in the middle of the night just when I would finally drift off to sleep. I was so hungry but they only brought me salty bouillon, which I didn't drink, instead of the broth the doctor had ordered. Wednesday night the surgeon who was scheduled to remove the stone came in and said that he didn't think I would need their services because I apparently had passed the stone! Praise God! I was so relieved as we have a dear friend who almost died several times from infections after his bile duct had been cut in surgery. He will likely be on antibiotics for the rest of his life. So once again prayer was answered. However, I was still scheduled for the gall bladder and hernia operations on Friday. Late Thursday night they came in and told me that they were taking me down for a two-hour sonogram. I said,

"Why two hours? I just had a 20-minute one last night?"

He said they needed to be sure that I had in fact passed the stone. Otherwise, if the doctor got in there and found that it was still blocking things, he would have to revert to the old way of doing that kind of operation, from which it takes much longer to recuperate. It was so quiet with just the technician and me, but I fought off the sleep and, praise the Lord, the stone <u>was</u> gone! I got just a little sleep before they came in to check my vitals and to draw more blood.

Friday morning, Bud, our daughters, and a granddaughter were there before the surgery, and I was pleasantly surprised to also see our new young visitation pastor waiting to pray with us just before they sent me into la-la land. They have two young children and I was especially touched when I found out that their baby had cried most of the night and yet he still came so far to be with me early in the morning. Yes, I was very sick for two days, but I knew that would pass. On Saturday, I called Bud and asked him not to come until that evening, and, when he did, to 'sneak me in' some real mashed potatoes from Boston Market. I thought that perhaps I would stop vomiting if I just had something to eat. I begged the doctor for some food, so he finally consented to let me have some plain crackers, but when Bud came that evening I devoured those mashed potatoes! They finally fed me on Sunday and I was able to come home later that afternoon. I was very weak, but at least I was home. Our youngest daughter, Candy, brought her 10-year-old daughter, Brigitta, who had been so worried about her grandma. We are so close. I saw the concern on her face as she said,

"Oh Grandma, I was so worried about you and I prayed so hard!"

Candy said,

"I told her, 'Don't worry! Just pray for Grandma.'"

But she had to see for herself and have Grandma tell her that she was going to be all right.

When you are so sick, it is such a blessing to have precious family, friends, and pastors to pray for you and to know that God is right there—all the time.

Chapter 41
"We Can't Operate—too Dangerous!"

We arrived at Christian Retreat near the end of 2004 planning to stay until the following March 15th. I (Gertrude) had an appointment with a Florida surgeon who was going to do my partial knee resurfacing. I told him how sick I had gotten less than a year ago when they put me to sleep to remove my gall bladder, and that all pain medicines nauseate me. He said,

"Don't worry about it, we'll give you a spinal and find something that you can take for pain."

Then I went into the hospital for my pre-op on January 6th in preparation for the knee surgery on the 7th. After the pre-op procedures, the nurse came in and asked if I had ever had a stroke.

"No," I answered.

She asked, "Have you ever had any hemorrhages?"

Again I answered, "No."

She continued, "Any blood clots?"

"Not to my knowledge," I answered.

Then she asked if I had had any recent blood tests, so I gave her the name of my family doctor back in Ohio, and two Ohio hospitals where I recalled they drew blood from me for gall bladder surgery back in March of 2004.

Several hours passed when a doctor came in and said,

> "You will not be having your knee surgery tomorrow. Your blood platelets are over a million and we do not operate unless they are 400,000 maximum, and preferably even lower. We will be moving you down a floor for further tests."

(The Orthopedic center had the whole top suite where I was staying.)

That was Thursday, so Friday I was moved down one floor for more tests. They spent all Friday night pumping two pints of blood into me. (Sunday I found out that I hadn't needed it. I did not appreciate that as my veins are so tiny that by then both arms were black and blue.)

The hematologist came Saturday morning and did a bone marrow biopsy, and said that his partner would be seeing me Sunday. In the meantime, I asked for a printout of my blood tests and so when his partner came on Sunday, I asked him how my hemoglobin could jump from 7.4 on Thursday to 18.1 on Saturday after just two pints of blood. He literally ran out of that room. When he returned he told me what had happened—my blood was so thick that the lab technician had thinned it to run the tests, so they thought that I needed more blood. [The other tests were fine using the thinned sample, the hemoglobin number being the only piece of data that was affected.] He apologized, and I imagine he read the riot act to the lab people.

He then told us that he suspected I had Essential Thrombocythemia, which in layman's terms means that my blood makes too many platelets. He said that it was not cancer, but they would still be treating it with a chemo drug to bring the platelet number down. He gave me a few tablets and wrote me a prescription to take three tablets a day, discharged me, and asked me to come back Thursday to his oncology office when they would have the results of the bone marrow biopsy. So we returned to *Christian Retreat* Sunday afternoon.

Monday morning I called numerous pharmacies before I found one that stocked the special prescription. I did not get the entire prescription filled, as it would have cost over $500.00. Rather, I got only enough to last until Thursday when I had to go back to the hematologist. On Thursday I told him that we could not afford that drug, so he wrote a prescription for another one, but it had more potential side effects. We prayed about that and (forgive me for being so vain) also asked the Lord to keep me from losing my hair. [I didn't lose any of my hair! Thank you Lord!]

We made the 100-mile round trip from *Christian Retreat* to the hematologist in Largo until the platelets had dropped low enough for the knee surgery to be done, which I then had on February 14th. Though they gave me a spinal, they told me that because I had begun moving around on the operating table during surgery, they had to put me to sleep. Consequently, I was sick after the surgery, but they still sent me home the next day. Those of you who have had knee surgery know the severity of the pain, but added to that were my medication problems, which included nausea and diarrhea. I knew that I had to do the physical therapy exercises, or the operation would have been in vain. Precious friends from all over the U.S. and Canada that were staying at the Retreat visited and prayed for me, as well as family and friends back home.

Since Ohio was experiencing a bad winter, I wanted to stay in Florida until the 15th of March as we had initially planned, but Bud wanted to get me back home. At his insistence, I made reservations to fly home a few days earlier on March 10th. I was thankful when Bud's youngest sister, who was wintering in Lakeland, decided to accompany me on the flight home. Bud drove me to their home in Lakeland, and caught a few hours of sleep before he headed back to Archbold alone in our car. The next afternoon my brother-in-law drove his wife (Bud's sister) and me to the airport for the flight back to Ohio. Our youngest daughter, Candy, drove through a snowstorm to pick us up in Toledo. I could hardly believe it, but what a surprise (and relief) to see the lights on when we drove into our driveway! Bud had driven straight through from Florida, catching a little break now and then at some rest areas on the way. God had seen him safely through a lot of snow and one close call. There is no place like home and your own bed.

I pushed myself a little more each day and, as the drug dosage was lowered, I gained more strength. I went to church on Easter Sunday, and as soon as the snow was gone I was outside working for short periods.

By the middle of April, I was walking the long hallways with Bud at the jail to conduct our usual Sunday morning services.

I was determined to play golf with my ladies' league when it started at the end of May, so I golfed a few holes with Bud the week before the league started. As I am one who has always been so active, I thought to myself,

"Why did I tire so easily after only nine holes?"

But I did not give up, and neither should you if you are going through difficult circumstances. I just kept planting flowers, weeding, and doing my work little by little, and praising God each time new flowers came out. In July, as the temperatures climbed into the 90s, I was at the golf course three times a week with Bud by 7 A.M. getting in 18 holes before it got too hot. Do I still get tired? Yes, some days more than others. Today I golfed the best with my ladies' league that I have for years, having four pars in a row! WOW. I had never done that before.

I am thankful that I quit putting off having my knee surgery done or we would not have known about the blood disorder to even pray about it. The hematologist in Florida told me that I would be on this medication for the rest of my life, but we are praying about that also. As of this writing, I have gone from 21 chemo pills a week down to 6, and the platelets have stayed within a normal range. I am praying that he will be able to cut the dosage even further. When I was in so much pain after the surgery trying to do my exercises, I thought,

"Why did I have this done?"

But it is so wonderful now to be able to go up and down my basement steps.

I had been waiting for God to heal my knee without surgery, which He certainly could have done, but He had other plans. Bud stayed in a room at the hospital both times I was there, and he not only got to witness to staff but to a lot of people who were coming in for surgery. Also, those weeks that we sat in the oncology waiting room, we both spoke to a lot of people and saw how much better off I was than most of the patients. Bad things happen to all of us, but years ago I determined never to walk any valleys in vain. I always want to try to fulfill God's purpose for allowing me to go through such valleys, knowing that He is right there with me when I pray.

Chapter 42
"The Case of the Lost Camera"

A few days before I (Gertrude) was to have my knee surgery, some friends invited Bud and me to meet them at their place and ride with them to a seafood restaurant for lunch. Since we expected to go on to Venice, as we had done before, Bud wanted to take along our digital camera. After Bud went out to the car, he decided that he might need a jacket since we would be by the water, so he laid the camera up on the trunk of the car, and went back into the house to get his jacket. When he returned a few minutes later, he walked right past the camera and got into the car. I just got into my side as I knew nothing about the camera. Since we didn't go on to Venice after we ate, he didn't miss the camera until we returned to our friend's place. We searched both cars for the camera before Bud remembered what had happened. We then immediately returned to our place and slowly drove up and down the boulevard there as well as up and down the roads leading out to Interstate 75.

Bud said that because the camera had been on the driver's side of the trunk lid, it probably would have flown off of the trunk to the center of the road and smashed into a million pieces. Even if it hadn't, it certainly seemed like it would have been run over on I-75 where cars literally fly by. I refused to accept that possibility and prayed for God to somehow see to it that we got the camera back. [It was very special to us, as it was a Christmas gift from our children.] When I asked others to pray with us that we would get the camera back, Bud reminded me that even if someone did find it, our local Florida address was not on the camera case. [He did have his name, town, and our Ohio telephone number on the case, but we had turned off our answering machine in Ohio when we left.]

Several days went by with no news about our missing camera. The van from the orthopedic center was to pick us up at 11:00 A.M. to take us to Largo Medical Center where I was having my right knee operated on the next day. We just had time to attend the early service at *Christian Retreat* where we were staying. At the end of the service, communion was served at the front of the church. As we were waiting our turn, Pastor Phil came down off the platform and walked up to us. He very quietly said,

"Bud, I have your camera in my car."

I said,

"I just knew that we would get it back!"

Astonished, Bud said,

"Where did you find it?"

Phil answered,

"My neighbor found it when he was out walking. It had your name and Archbold, Ohio on the case so he brought it to me." He said, "I know that you know a lot of people from all over. Do you know this man?"

Of course Pastor Phil knew us, as we had owned one side of a duplex at *Christian Retreat* for nine years and both of us did a lot of volunteer work there. Bud told him that we were leaving shortly for the hospital and that we would like to take it along, so Pastor Phil slipped out to his car and brought the camera to us. After communion we returned to the duplex that we were staying at and got a bite to eat just before the van arrived.

Once again, I had a pre-op procedure that verified my blood platelets had come down to a level where it was safe for me to have the operation. So, the next day, which was Valentine's Day, I had the knee surgery and returned to *Christian Retreat* the next evening where I was to do my own rehab. I was very sick, but, because the pain medicine did not agree with me, I decided to take it only at night so I could get some sleep. I depended on the help of my good husband and the prayers of many friends. As I did the necessary rehab exercises, I prayed the whole while as I fought back the tears and nausea.

Due to this set of medical circumstances, Bud didn't really have the time to get back to the man who had found the camera. When we were given his name and where he lived, Bud went over to thank him and to offer him a reward, which he refused. Later, Bud took the man one of his handcrafted putters that he makes. The man admitted that he had given the camera to his daughters, who immediately said,

"Dad, we can't keep this, it belongs to this man."

That is when he took it to Pastor Phil. Thank God that the Holy Spirit not only spoke to his daughters, but also told the man where to take it so we would get it back. Once again God answers prayer!

Chapter 43
"Be Ready!"

The Word tells us that we are to be ready "in season and out of season" to tell about the hope that is within us (II Timothy 4:2). No matter what the situation is, we should be ready to talk about Jesus and his love. Early one Monday morning, I decided to play a round of golf. Where we are members, our golf course does not require tee times so I went directly to the first tee. When I got there, a man with whom I had previously played was also there, so I asked him to ride along with me in my cart.

The morning before, Gertrude and I did the Sunday morning service at the five county correctional center where miraculous things happened. I was relating these things to Frank, my golfing partner, as we went from green to green. When we reached the fourth tee, we each hit our ball and then headed out in the cart for our second shot. At that time I could still out-drive Frank, so I drove first to Frank's ball for him to hit. He walked over, addressed his ball, but just stood there, not moving for about 10 seconds. Without hitting his ball he came back to the cart and sat down. I said,

"You want to know Jesus don't you?

At this he said,

"Yes, I do!"

It was my privilege to introduce him to Jesus that morning.

We since have become very good friends, and at the time of this writing Frank has recovered from surgery. Of course we prayed for both him and the surgeon several times before his surgery. One of those prayers was said right on the golf course while golfing with my good friend Lowell, who is also a brother in Christ. We came upon Frank and his foursome and just had a short prayer with him, as we didn't want to make a spectacle of ourselves. They had plans to remove Frank's gallbladder along with other surgery, but God must have taken care of that because they found there was no longer a need to remove the gallbladder. Frank was soon back on the golf course, first just chipping and putting, but we praised God for answering prayer.

Another time a few years ago, I was golfing in a senior's scramble, and a friend who is a few years older than I was on my team and riding with me. He was a good golfer but cancer had taken its toll on him and his body was becoming weaker and more frail, making it difficult for him whenever he hit the ball. As we came to the last hole, I asked him if it was all right for me to pray for that cancer problem. He said, "Yes," and so I just asked the Lord in a simple way to remove the cancer. Over the next few weeks his body returned to normal and that has been about 10 years ago. He still golfs, but not as much as he used to because of his age. I am relating these stories as a way of encouraging believers to be ready at all times, because you never know when or where God will bring someone into your life with a need, and it is up to you/us to pray for that need. I ask the question—"If we don't pray for those needs, who will?" Once again, I reference John 14:12 where Jesus says, "Anyone who has faith in me will do what I have been doing." I firmly believe that if we practice that, it will make a big difference in the world around us.

Some time ago I went to play golf and, as I approached the first tee, I saw a man that I casually knew standing there alone. I asked him if he wanted to play along with me, which invitation he gladly accepted. As we drove from tee to tee, the Holy Spirit led me to talk about the Lord, which I am not always directed to do. When we had finished golfing, I drove him to his car. He started to put his clubs into the trunk and I headed to the cart barn, but went only about 50 yards when the Holy Spirit said,

"Go back. He is ready to receive Christ."

I went back just as he was finishing putting his equipment into the trunk, so I asked,

"Do you want to ask Jesus into your life as your Lord and Savior?"

"Yes," he replied, and right there in front of an open trunk he received Jesus as his Savior.

Occasionally God will bring an incident to our minds that may have happened years ago just to encourage us. About a year ago I was using my credit card to check out at a home improvement store. I signed my legal name—Otis Hitt. [My mother was so sure that I was going to be another girl that she promised an uncle of mine that if I was a boy she would name me after him, Otis. Much to her surprise I was not a girl, but she kept her promise and named me Otis, but said, "He will always be Buddie." So I received my nickname "Bud" at birth.] The clerk looked at my signature, then at me, and asked,

"Are you Bud Hitt?"

"Yes." I replied.

Then she said,

"Do you remember me? I'm Barbara. You and your wife led me to the Lord about 20 years ago and I have been walking with Him ever since."

Then I remembered her and, since there was no one else in line, we reminisced and rejoiced together. God is so good.

Chapter 44
"Stay Away!"

    I wasn't going to write this story but was urged by the Holy Spirit to include it just as it happened.

    On a Sunday morning, about a year ago as of this writing, Gertrude led the men in singing at the jail and, as she always does, ended with a prayer. I was sitting with my head down and eyes closed when suddenly I had a vision that lasted only about 15 seconds. In the vision I was in Toledo, which is about 60 miles east from where I was sitting. I saw myself driving down a main street where I came to a familiar intersection, one that I had passed many times in the days of delivering trophies when we were in business. In my vision, I looked off to my left and it seemed like I could see two large houses where I somehow discerned that people went for drugs. Though I had passed that intersection many times, I had never actually driven down the street that I saw in my vision off to the left. I know that you can't see those particular houses from that intersection, but somehow I could see them clearly in this vision. Then I was given a message to warn the men. After Gertrude had finished praying, I stood up and related to them what I had just seen. Immediately two men held up their hands and said that everything that I described was true and that they knew where those crack houses were. I proceeded to give all of the men the warning that they were never to go there or they might lose their life. It was difficult for me to tell them this, but I did it because I knew that, in his love, God was warning someone. When I receive these Words of Knowledge [one of the Gifts of the Spirit] I don't know all the details of what I'm talking about, but whomever it's meant for certainly does.

This was in the fall and we soon went to Florida. When we returned to Ohio in the spring, we resumed the Sunday morning services at the jail. I related this story in the men's service and a man in the front row held up his hand to speak. He said that he happened to be in the service when that Word of Knowledge was given. One of the men who knew about the crack houses did not heed the warning and, when released, returned to them and did in fact lose his life. God loves us all so much that he doesn't want us to perish but, rather, to live the abundant life.

Chapter 45
"What Boils?"

In 2004, we started having two other volunteers, Dick, and his wife Violet, go with us on Sunday mornings for services at the jail. Dick and Violet had "white passes" which allowed them to bring the inmates to our services so that we did not have to wait for a movement officer, thus allowing us more time to minister.

One Sunday morning, prior to us doing either of our services, our friend Dick asked us to pray for him. He had been observing us praying for the inmates and had a need of his own for which he wanted us to pray. He had some painful boils under his arm, limiting the ability to raise his arm. He had an appointment with the doctor again who was going to incise them. We simply asked the Lord to heal those boils in Jesus' name. A few days later, Dick and his wife returned to the doctor who, after having Dick raise his arm, said,

"Show me where they are."

Dick's wife had been keeping them cleansed for him so Dick asked her to show the doctor where they were. But the boils were no longer there! God had healed him! The following Sunday Dick gave that testimony to the inmates to encourage them. Once again, it was God who healed him in the Name of Jesus.

On November 1, 2004 Dick was killed in a car accident on his way home after working on arrangements for a special program at the jail.

This came as a terrible shock to all of us. We are so glad Violet had family that helped her in her time of grief. We feel privileged to have shared the last few months of Dick's life and to have watched him grow in the Lord. Since Dick's death, God has provided another precious couple that is going with us to the jail, who will take our place when we are in Florida.

Chapter 46
"Respond to a Hurting World"

After we had friends over to our house recently, I started thinking that people may think as they read this book that we have special power to reach God in a way that they cannot. As I stated previously in the book, we are just ordinary children of God who try to share Jesus every chance we get. It is really only through the power of God that these wonderful things happen. Jesus told us that, if we ask in His Name, it will be done. When we receive Jesus into our life, we receive the right to use His name. That is why Jesus said in Acts 1:8, "You shall receive power when the Holy Spirit comes upon you." Again, quoting John 14:12, "Anyone who has faith in me will do what I have been doing." Search your Bible and see what Jesus was doing. As His representatives, we are to share the love of Christ and His offer of salvation through His blood, and simply pray for a hurting world. Each of us lives in our own little world and it is up to us to respond to the needs of those around us. Even though my wife and I live mainly in the same little world, she sees people that I may never meet, and I come in contact with people that she may never meet. The important thing is to respond to those situations that God brings to each of us.

Sometimes the need for which we are praying is greater than our faith at that moment, but we always have that 'mustard seed' of faith. Use the faith that you have and ask with confidence, always in the Name of

Jesus, and leave the results up to God. It is all right to ask God to increase our faith so that we don't ask "wavering." A stanza from the old hymn *"What a friend we have in Jesus,"* says, "Oh, what needless pain we bear. All because we do not carry, everything to God in prayer." Jesus spoke of those with <u>no</u> faith, those with <u>little</u> faith and those with <u>great</u> faith. Through a proper prayer life, we want to be in the latter category.

We are to pray for those in authority, from our President down to the local level of government. 1st Timothy 2:2 tells us that we should pray for those in authority, so that we may lead a quiet and peaceable life in all godliness and honesty. There is a hurting world out there with many spiritual, emotional, and physical needs. We, who call God our Father and Jesus Christ our Savior, must reach out to them, pray for them, and encourage them in the faith. There are also discouraged Christians out there who need to be strengthened in their inner beings. So often I have heard Gertrude tell the inmates that the prayer of Ephesians 3:14-21 is what she wants for them; namely, "To be strengthened in their inner man so as to really know the power of His love." She goes on to tell them that to really know Christ, and the <u>fullness</u> of His love, we have to know His Word by studying the Bible and praying. When I am sharing Christ with someone, I always stress the point that they should read the Gospel of John, Chapters 14, 15, 16, and 17 over and over until the words sink deep into their spirit. When these chapters get into your spirit, the Bible suddenly becomes alive. You will get excited anticipating what God has planned for you for each day. An example of this is what happened at our place of business one day.

While we were in business we had many opportunities to share Christ. One day when I was busy working on a particular layout, a man from whom I had bought a lot of walnut lumber over the years came in to see me. He began talking about his retirement from the lumber business and the heartbreak of losing his wife after many years of marriage. I listened as he poured out his loneliness. When he finished, I expressed to him my sympathy and told him that my wife was also my best earthly friend, but then I asked him if he knew my <u>very</u> best friend—Jesus.

He responded,

"Not the way that you do, even though I have been a church member all my life."

I then proceeded to introduce him to Jesus. Gertrude was in her office and, overhearing our conversation, she started to pray. She came out and joined us, and the three of us rejoiced over his salvation. We asked the Lord to heal his broken heart and to fill his lonely hours. John was from another state and quite elderly, which is probably why we never saw him again, but he left with a peace in his heart that day that I'm sure sustained him over the following weeks and months.

Chapter 47
"For God So Loved The World"

The Word does not say that God loves only the USA, or even our own church group, but that He loves the <u>whole</u> world, even with all the evil in it. We should not isolate ourselves in our own little groups but, rather, we are to represent the Lord wherever we are. It is great to get together with our Christian friends, but we must be careful not to become cliquish to the point of ignoring those who need the fellowship of Christians.

Many people are hurting and need prayer. Many of those try to fill their lives with things that don't really satisfy their emptiness, such as alcohol. I remember when we were wintering at Sun City in South Carolina, I went to the clubhouse to get one of those "Friday night specials" carryout. They were busy serving drinks, as it was their "happy hour." While waiting for my order a lady said to me,

"We just came in this afternoon. What a wonderful place and what a wonderful happy hour."

Without thinking, I said,

"I was happy before I came in and I didn't need a drink to be happy."

She quickly walked away and I never got the chance to tell her why I was happy.

Perhaps I was too abrupt and had not earned the right to share more with her. We must walk in wisdom and follow the leading of the Holy Spirit, but not use that as an excuse to keep us from sharing the Lord with others when we have the opportunity.

We like to go out to eat at places where the emphasis is on food and not drinks. We have seen the heartache that drinking can cause. Jesus said that he didn't come to condemn the world, but to save it, so I do not want to condemn anyone. But the Bible also tells me that I am not to do anything that would cause someone else to stumble. That is one of the reasons that I do not wish to go into bars, as someone may see me and think that I approve of drinking. If so, they could misinterpret that action and possibly become an alcoholic and ruin their life and that of their loved ones. When I drive past a certain vacant lot where a tavern once stood where I spent many hours as a youth, I can almost see and hear the people who frequented that place. It is a strange feeling to see in my mind's eye the faces of those that have long been dead. After I became born again and gave my heart to the Lord, I never got drunk again. I never went back to it or any place like it. Thanks to Jesus, I am not the man I used to be!

Chapter 48
David's Healing

After selling our South Carolina winter home in April of 2002, and when it seemed like Ohio was getting even colder, Florida once again beckoned us. For the next four years we spent several months of the winter down there.

Long time friend, Eudora, had repeatedly urged us to buy a mobile home at Palmetto Mobile Home Club in Palmetto, Florida where she wintered. It is just across the bridge from Bradenton and close to Christian Retreat where my golfing Buddy, Hixon Pugh, lives year round. When Eudora once again invited us to stay with her one winter for as long as we wished, we accepted and spent almost three months with her in 2006. It wasn't long before we knew why so many of her friends from Illinois and Missouri, after visiting her, purchased mobile units there.

The park has 475 units that are co-op owned, so no owner needs to be concerned that the ground will be sold out from under them. There are many activities and various clubs on site, such as a weekly Bible Study where Gertrude and I were invited to teach several times. Since there are a lot of Christians there, they have a hymn sing in the large clubhouse every Sunday night. We found out that a lot of folks from Ohio winter there who know Archbold fairly well, including where *Hit Trophy* business is located. The people there are so friendly and no one is a stranger. Eudora's neighbors and friends soon became our friends also, and we attended local Christian concerts together.

I began watching the weekly listings of the mobiles that came up for sale, and when the owners of a small mobile purchased a larger one, I convinced Gertrude that, since I am a woodworker and a jack-of-all trades, perhaps we should purchase this small fixer-upper. We prayed about it and decided on a price we would offer. We also asked the Lord that if we were not to buy it, the owner would not accept our offer. However, he accepted, so we purchased the unit and began renovating it.

In the meantime, one of Gertrude's sisters, Millie, had an accident back in Ohio. Gertrude spoke to her and prayed with her on the phone before her operation, which Millie survived, and the family was sure that she would fully recover. After a week of calling daily, Gertrude could no longer stand being so far away and said, "Tell Millie that we're heading home tonight." We drove straight through to Ohio, but Millie had gone to be with her Lord before we arrived. My wife was devastated, but so glad that she had spent a lot of fun time with Millie the previous summer. In her mind, she reviewed the spiritual talks they had together and recalled the time she took her instrument along and, above Millie's protests that she could no longer sing like she used to, insisted that they sing hymns together like they did in their teens. It was doubly hard losing her sister because Gertrude had just lost her last brother six weeks previously. She was not able to be there for his funeral because the ear specialist would not allow her to fly home from Florida due to an inner ear infection she had developed.

Gertrude had prayed for her brother Don for years, and her prayers were eventually answered. Before we left for Florida, we visited him several times a week, and in one of the last visits he repented and wept as we led him in a prayer of commitment to the Lord. On our last visit to Don, his daughter-in-law, who also had been praying for him, was there and happily said that he told her he had prayed with us. Due to smoking, Don was in and out of the hospital many times. He had lost half of his voice box and had to drag an oxygen tank around with him for years. Over and over he would say, as many do after it is too late, "Why did I ever start smoking?" In 2001 he had lost his twin brother to lung cancer.

Gertrude still misses them both, but takes consolation in the fact that Millie is no longer in pain and Don is no longer struggling to breathe. They are both with their parents and the rest of their siblings and relatives, which is most comforting.

Our dear friend David, who has put together this book for us, loves to spend time in Florida. He has a large van, so after Millie's funeral we left our car in Ohio and the three of us headed back to Florida in his van, which I loaded up with my tools, bicycle, a few pieces of furniture, and some woodworking materials from our local Sauder outlet store. His wife, Judy, had already purchased an airline ticket, planning to join him down in Florida a few weeks later for a short vacation, and then the four of us planned to drive back to Ohio together.

We had junked the furnace, stove, and most of the furniture that was in the mobile, but thankfully there was a good bed there for David to sleep in since we were still staying at Eudora's. We arrived late Friday night, March 3rd, unloaded Saturday morning, and went to the Gospel Jamboree at *Christian Retreat* that night. Sunday after church we relaxed, but on Monday I started in again renovating the unit while David painted the bedroom. The next morning when I got to our mobile, David was in excruciating pain in his back. Gertrude and I prayed for him, but when there seemed to be no relief we took him to Blake Memorial hospital for X-rays, which revealed nothing out of the ordinary. The doctor gave him a RX for pain and said that sometimes just a sneeze can put your back out. We returned to the mobile, and the next morning, when his back was no better, Gertrude booked a direct flight for him to Ohio. In the meantime, his wife had made an appointment for him with their local doctor who, after examining David, immediately scheduled him for an appointment with a neurosurgeon in Toledo. David had a lumbar MRI, which revealed a cyst-type of mass in his spinal canal. As soon as the neurosurgeon had an opening in his surgery schedule, he said that he would operate on David.

Until then, David was assigned to a local physical therapist, and after several weeks of therapy his back began to feel better. Since Judy had already purchased her ticket to fly down, David purchased one for himself so he could come back to Florida with her. While he was up north taking care of his physical needs, I had about two weeks to replace a wall, seal some leaks, put up new paneling, lay new vinyl and carpet, and hook up a new stove before they returned. Gertrude cleaned up after me and put dishes and things that we had brought from Ohio into the cupboards. Even though it was only for a short time that they would be there, we wanted it to be a nice vacation for them. After David and Judy arrived, I continued to work in the unit but did not finish the lanai or patio. I filled our little on-site shed with my tools and materials until our return in the fall, and the four of us headed north to Ohio.

When we return to Florida this fall, the lanai is first thing on the agenda, as our daughter, Dawn, is looking forward to spending the month of February 2007 with us. We will give the master bedroom to her and we will sleep on trundle beds in the lanai. Ohio winters are difficult for her, so we would appreciate your prayers for her continued healing.

Upon returning to Ohio, and before they could operate on David's back, he ended up in St. Vincent's Hospital in Toledo with bladder complications. After doing both jail services on Easter, Gertrude and I went to the hospital to visit David (and Judy) and to pray for him. The following Wednesday night we went to Toledo again and took the Rose's, a couple from our Bible Study with us. All of us believe in divine healing and agreed together in prayer for David's healing. David later told us, "During that prayer time, Bud laid his hand on me and prayed for the cyst to be removed, which I thought was a little odd since my problem at the time was my bladder. I felt that I was healed right then through that spirit-led focused prayer."

After a few weeks, David went back to his neurosurgeon with no pain. The surgeon, somewhat surprised, scheduled a second MRI to try to ascertain what had changed. To our delight, the follow-up MRI revealed that the cyst was gone! The report of the radiologist contained the summary comment, "No evidence of the previous posterior spinal mass at L3-L4." All we can say is, thank you Heavenly Father for answered prayer, and thank you, Jesus, for giving us the power that is in YOUR NAME to use when we pray. I know that many other people were praying for David and his bladder complications, and we are praying and believing that those problems will not return.

The weather is cooling, school has started, and David is teaching some classes at a local college, but I remember the many times in the summer, as the birds sang and the squirrels chased each other around our yard, that David and I sat on our enclosed back porch and talked about the Bible and God. As I glance across the farmlands that border our back yard and think about the things of God that we do not understand, such as why some people are healed and some are not, I know that God is sovereign and so I leave the answers to Him in every prayer that I pray.

One thing I do understand is that God still answers the prayers of ordinary people when we ask in faith and in the Name of Jesus.

Healing is a gift
Bestowed by God on man;
One of God's pleasures is
To see us use it in His plan.

If you have compassion
Of God's healing power thru you,
Speak God's Word and bless those in need
And watch what His power will do.

So many people came to Jesus
To be healed by His own Hand;
He sent His disciples to recruit workers,
As they went throughout the land.

God sends the gift of healing
To people just like you;
How blessed you are in helping
Those who are suffering and now made new.

The harvest is so great
And the workers are so few;
Pray to Him in charge, to recruit
More ordinary people just like you.

By
Marla J. Starry

Printed in the United States
75034LV00003B/1-108